Smithsonian
Cooper-Hewitt, National Design Museum
NEW YORK

COLOR MOVES:
ART & FASHION BY
SONIA
DELAUNAY

EDITED BY

MATILDA MCQUAID AND SUSAN BROWN

WITH CONTRIBUTIONS BY

MATTEO DE LEEUW-DE MONTI

PETRA TIMMER

FOREWORD

BILL MOGGRIDGE, DIRECTOR,
CAROLINE BAUMANN, ASSOCIATE DIRECTOR,
COOPER-HEWITT, NATIONAL DESIGN MUSEUM

"In about 1911, I had the idea of making for my son, who had just been born, a blanket composed of bits of fabric like those I had seen in the houses of Russian peasants. When it was finished, the arrangement of the pieces of material seemed to me to evoke Cubist conceptions, and we then tried to apply the same process to other objects and paintings."

Sonia Delaunay said this about a patchwork quilt that she made for the crib of her infant son Charles. The "we" she refers to included her husband, Robert, about whom she said, "In Robert Delaunay I found a poet — a poet who wrote not with words but with colors." Their collaboration lasted until Robert's death thirty years later, but Sonia continued her creative explorations of color and form in paintings, textile design, stage-set design, book design, and the application of color and shape to the surfaces of objects. She was fascinated in the power of juxtaposed colors to come alive, creating an impression of movement. She also had a flair for fashion and a nimble vocabulary of descriptive words that gave her choices of color additional vibrancy. The excellence of her work was recognized in 1964, when she was chosen to be the first living female artist and designer to have a retrospective exhibition at Paris's Musée du Louvre.

Sonia grew up in the care of her uncle's family in St. Petersburg, Russia, who provided an adequate stipend for her and Robert to live in Paris as they developed their artistic ideas. But the Russian Revolution put a sudden end to that carefree way of life, causing Sonia to open her own design practice, called Casa Sonia, in Madrid, designing clothing, interiors, and costumes for ballet while Robert continued painting. Eventually, the Delaunays returned to Paris, where the Dada movement was in full swing, and added their own "Simultaneist" experiments to the mix. Sonia's success with designs for costumes and fashion allowed her to open her own business, Maison Delaunay, in 1925, and gradually her fame spread, especially for her fabric designs. The economic

Tissu simultané no. 60.
France, 1924. Block-printed on cotton velveteen.
Musée de l'Impression sur Étoffes, Mulhouse, 980.528.2

Rythme no. 5. France,
1939. Gouache on paper.
Private collection

crash of 1929 put a hold on the growth of her practice, but her textile designs became a staple in the 1930s, under the trademark Tissus Delaunay. It was in this period that she first started working with the Metz & Co department store in Amsterdam, leading to a long-term collaboration with Joseph de Leeuw and his son Hendrik. You will find an interesting description of this relationship in the essays that follow by Matteo de Leeuw-de Monti, grandson of Joseph and son of Hendrik, as well as rich details of her career as designer and artist in the essay by Delaunay historian Petra Timmer. Matilda McQuaid, Deputy Curatorial Director and Head of the Textiles department at Cooper-Hewitt, who co-curated this exhibition with Associate Textiles Curator Susan Brown, contributes an introduction.

Nearly thirty years have passed since Sonia Delaunay's work has been presented by a major museum in the United States. *Color Moves: Art and Fashion by Sonia Delaunay* focuses on her textiles and fashion work primarily from the 1920s through the 1940s, when she explored intensively the relationships between design and art, movement and color. We have been very fortunate to have the support of Jean-Louis Delaunay, grandson of Sonia and Robert, from the inception of the Color Moves project. France's Musée des Arts Décoratifs, Musée de la Mode de la Ville de Paris, and Musée de l'Impression sur Étoffes

de Mulhouse, along with private collectors in Europe and the United States, have generously lent their remarkable Delaunay creations to this exhibition and book. When seen together, they show the extraordinary range of her work. In particular, we are extremely grateful to Matteo de Leeuw-de Monti, who made available not only a beautiful collection of Delaunay designs and textiles, but also drawings by other important designers commissioned by Metz & Co during the 1930s.

We would also like to thank all the contributors whose generosity has helped to make this exhibition possible, including The Horace W. Goldsmith Foundation, The Coby Foundation, Ltd., The Anna-Maria and Stephen Kellen Foundation, the Ehrenkranz Fund, and the Esme Usdan Exhibition Endowment Fund. Additional support for which we are most grateful as well was provided by the Josef and Anni Albers Foundation, Lisa S. Roberts, the Consulate-General of The Netherlands, and The Felicia Fund. This beautiful publication is supported in part by The Andrew W. Mellon Foundation, with additional funding from Furthermore: a program of the J. M. Kaplan Fund. We hope that this color extravaganza of over 300 textiles, designs, clothing, and accessories that the organizations above have helped make possible will inspire another generation of designers.

INTRODUCTION

MATILDA MCQUAID

Sonia Delaunay was a modern artist and designer who merged art and everyday life. Her work encompassed everything from paintings and drawings, painted ceramics, and neon light sculpture to posters, textiles, and costume designs (FIG. 1). Committed to transforming the world through color, she designed dresses and coats, illustrated books, and painted scarves and canvases with equal fervor (FIG. 8). No article of clothing, furnishing, or interior escaped her notion of "color as the skin of the world."[1] It was color alone that created the virtual movement in her work, reflecting the age of modernity and its technological innovations — electric streetlights, airplanes, cars, and industrial machinery — which inspired her artistically.

In 1912, she and her husband, painter Robert Delaunay, formulated their own principles about color expressed through simultaneity — the sensation of movement when placing contrasting colors side by side. There were more theoretical interpretations of simultaneism which related to the collapse of time, and the idea that traditionally disharmonious elements can create harmonious relationships.[2] Exact meaning varied from artist to artist, including writers and poets, but with Sonia Delaunay it was about transforming ordinary colors into provocative forms that moved (FIG. 2). In the first two decades of her career, she exercised principles of simultaneity in all media, and with an intuitive approach that began in 1911 (a year earlier than Robert Delaunay's theory of simultaneity) with the colorful patchwork quilt she made for her newborn son, Charles. Delaunay constructed the quilt, a collage of different colors and textured fabrics cut out in a variety of geometric shapes, like her designs for book covers and textiles in subsequent years and decades.

As Delaunay so often remarked, there was no difference between her painting and design work. For her, working with textiles, books, and other useful objects meant free expansion, a conquest of new spaces.[3] Especially during the 1920s and 1930s, she approached different media similarly, whether it was a design for a textile, painting, or gouache. She created form, both figurative and abstract, through color.

One of Delaunay's most important works during the 1910s was the collaboration with the poet Blaise Cendrars on *La prose du Transsibérien et de la petite Jehanne de France*, an account of a young poet's train journey from Moscow to the Sea of Japan (FIGS. 4–6). Planned as an edition of 150 (only sixty-two were actually assembled), the text was printed in four colors and several different font sizes on a single sheet of paper that folded accordion-style into twenty-two panels. To the left of center were Delaunay's "illuminations," created with a *pochoir*, or handmade stencil, which offered controllability of form and the freedom of hand-coloring. Different color arcs, concentric half-circles, and amoeboid-like forms nestled against each, creating a prismatic patterning that complemented the text to the

FIG. 1. Sonia Delaunay in her studio at boulevard Malesherbes, Paris, France, 1925. Photographed by Germaine Krull. Bibliothèque Nationale de France, Paris

right of center. Splotches of colors bled into Cendrars's text from the right margins, surrounding and accentuating the words and lines which created their own form. This two-meter long synergy of color and text ended with a reference to and images of the Eiffel Tower and a Ferris wheel, famous symbols of modern Paris. In fact, the intention was that the complete edition would reach to the top of the Eiffel Tower when laid end to end.[4] When the illustrated poem was introduced in October 1913, the poet Guillaume Apollinaire said, "Cendrars and Madame Delaunay-Terk have realized a unique experiment in simultaneity, written in contrasts of colors in order to train the eye to read with one glance the whole of a poem, as an orchestra conductor reads with one glance the notes placed up and down the bar, as one sees with a single glance the plastic elements printed on a poster."[5] A decade later, Delaunay achieved this same sensibility in the printed silk and embroidered dress that was a receptacle for layers of color and texture, bound together with shimmering metallic embroidery (FIG. 7).

Delaunay continued to experiment with color and image in graphic design after her collaboration with Cendrars. She explored poster designs for Pirelli tires, Zenith watches, Bensdorf chocolate, and Dubonnet wine, melding color, image, and words to such an extreme that only a letter or two was decipherable (FIG. 3). Although impractical for advertising, they were true to her sensibility for color and movement. Her cover designs for publications such as *Les Arts Plastiques* (FIG. 11) more clearly displayed the title, and in this instance virtually replicated a textile she designed almost one year earlier when she established her atelier for printing simultaneous fabrics in 1924 (FIG. 10).

In this catalogue, essays by Petra Timmer and Matteo de Leeuw-de Monti examine Delaunay's most prodigious period of textile design. Timmer explains the importance of textiles for Delaunay's career beginning in the 1910s through the 1930s, relating how they were the primary medium for Delaunay's experimentation with color during this time as well as a key source of income which sustained her family through two world wars. Commissions from architects, designers, actresses, and other celebrities

FIG. 2. *Projet de tissu simultané (Design for Simultaneous Textile) no. 6.* France, 1924. Watercolor on paper. Les Arts Décoratifs, Paris, 40393

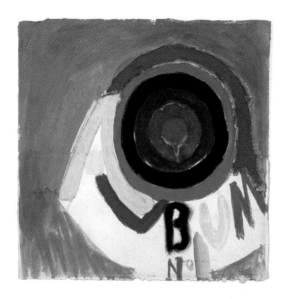

presented her with artistic and financial opportunities after she returned to Paris in 1920 to set up an atelier. Her move was timely: Paris was the capital of the world of fashion, which during the 1920s became the means by which women demonstrated their independence through simplified styles, loose clothing, and the popular "Joan of Arc" bob cut (FIG. 13). Nothing captures the spirit of the modern woman better than this model, cigarette in hand, dressed in pajamas designed by Delaunay, casually sitting inside a room designed by avant-garde designers Pierre Chareau and Francis Jourdain with Robert Mallet-Stevens for the 1925 *Exposition des Arts Décoratifs* in Paris (FIG. 9). The fashionably dressed woman was also linked to the new consumer plaything of the decade—the automobile.[6] By the 1920s, women were pictured behind the wheel, creating a visual image of female mobility and power, which became all the more colorful and dynamic through Delaunay's creations (FIG. 12).

De Leeuw-de Monti's personal recollection of Delaunay continues the textile story through the 1940s. He recounts her longstanding relationship with his family and Metz & Co, the celebrated Dutch

FIG. 3. *Album no. 1, no. 999.* France, 1916. Encaustic on paper. Private collection

FIG. 4. Cover for *La prose du Transsibérien et de la petite Jehanne de France.* France, 1913. Oil on leather. Courtesy of Barry Friedman and Patricia Pastor

FIG. 5. Pamphlet: *Prospectus La Prose du Transsibérien*. France, 1913. Gouache, pochoir (recto/verso). Collection of Antoine Blanchette

FIG. 6. *La prose du Transsibérien et de la petite Jehanne de France*. Text by Blaise Cendrars (Frédéric-Louis Sauser, French, born Switzerland, 1886–1961). Illustrated by Sonia Delaunay. Published by Éditions des Hommes Nouveaux. Paris, France, 1913. Illustrated book with pochoir, composition. Museum of Modern Art, New York 133.1951 A-B. Image © The Museum of Modern Art/Licensed by SCALA/Art Resource, New York

FIG. 7. Dress. France, 1925–28. Printed silk satin with metallic embroidery. Musée de la Mode de la Ville de Paris, Galliera, GAL 1970.58.31

department store and purveyors of avant-garde design. Joseph de Leeuw, owner and director of Metz & Co during the 1920s and 1930s, commissioned over 200 designs from Delaunay, which ranged from asymmetrical stripes and checks to brightly colored, raindrop-like forms and florals. Although different from her earlier forays in simultaneity, her work continued to be based in the language of color. Delaunay's design process during this period was carefully documented, from initial sketches and master prints to design cards, swatches, and final textile yardage. This invaluable collection of Metz textiles and designs, which De Leeuw-de Monti ultimately saved, researched, and catalogued, preserves an extraordinarily creative period relatively unknown until recently.

Crocodile, cactus, corinthe, and capucine[7] were some of the names that Sonia Delaunay gave to her colors, personalizing as well as organizing a palette which bestowed meaning to the words and images she painted and the textiles she designed. Color was her message, and her textiles wrapped the body in luminosity and form. The woman or man who donned a Delaunay garment wore a work of art, uncontained by a frame or an easel, but which stepped out into a life of independence and change. Thérèse Bonney's black-and-white photograph of a mannequin in a Delaunay scarf communicates texture, translucence, and contrast (FIG. 14). Delaunay's world may have been documented in black and white, but she reconceived it in color.

NOTES

1 Cohen, Arthur A., *Sonia Delaunay* (New York: Harry N. Abrams, 1975): 15.

2 Ibid., p. 29.

3 Delaunay, Sonia, *Nous irons jusqu'au soleil* (Paris: Editions Robert Laffont, 1978): 96.

4 Cohen, p. 31.

5 Ibid., p. 35.

6 Roberts, Mary Louise, "Samson and Delilah Revisited: The Politics of Fashion in 1920s France," in *The American Historical Review* (June 1993): 78.

7 Crocodile was beige to brown; cactus was green; corinthe was a shade of pink; and capucine a shade of orange.

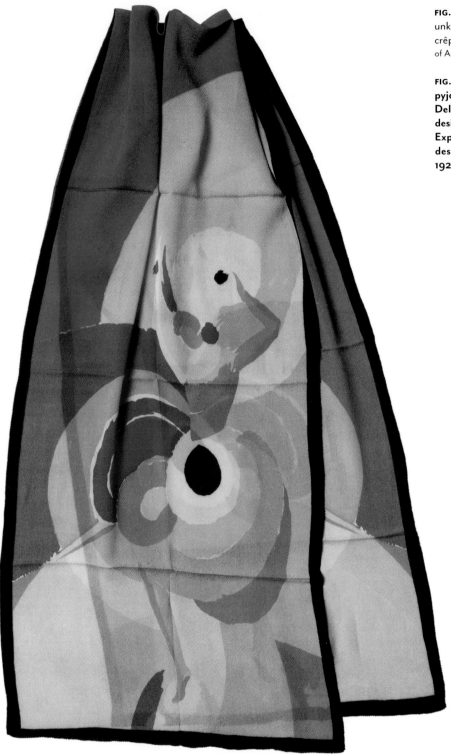

FIG. 8. Scarf. France, date unknown. Printed on silk crêpe de chine. Collection of Andrew Baseman

FIG. 9. Model wearing pyjama designed by Sonia Delaunay in interior designed by Pierre Chareau, Exposition Internationale des Arts Décoratifs, Paris, 1925. Private Collection

FIG. 10. *Projet de tissu simultané no. 34.* Blocks carved by Ferret. France, 1924. Watercolor on paper. Les Arts Décoratifs, Paris, 40397

FIG. 11. Pamphlet: *Les Arts Plastiques* (*The Plastic Arts*), **no. 2.** Cover illustration by Sonia Delaunay. France, 1925. Block-printed on paper. Collection of Antoine Blanchette

FIG. 12. Two models wearing Sonia Delaunay fashions with a Citroën B12 decorated by the artist, 1925. Bibliothèque Nationale de France, Paris

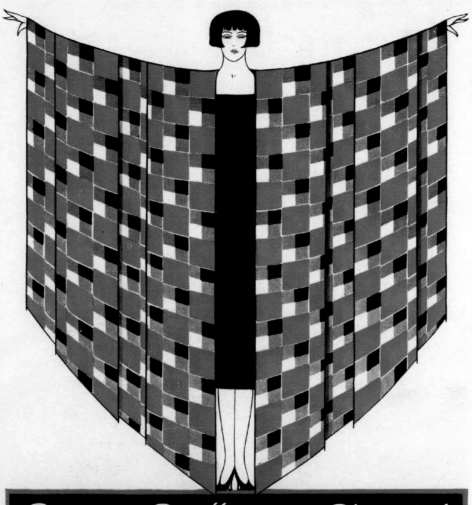

Godau_Guillaume_Arnault
12_Rue Ste Anne_PARIS
TISSUS Déposés
"SIMULTANÉ"

Le Gérant: M. BRUNHES. — Reg. du Com. de la Seine, Nᵒ 228.931.   Imp. de Vaugirard, Paris, (Encres Lorilleux.)

FIG. 13. Advertisement in
L'Officiel de la Mode, no. 44
(1925), p.73

FIG. 14. Siégel showroom
with mannequin designed
by René Herbst and
textile designed by Sonia
Delaunay, ca. 1926.
Photographed by Thérèse
Bonney. Smithsonian Institution
Libraries, V-977 MAN 031

SONIA DELAUNAY
FASHION AND
FABRIC DESIGNER

PETRA TIMMER

1946
Sonia
Delauné

"For me, there was no gap between my painting and what is called my 'decorative' work…. I never considered the 'minor arts' to be artistically frustrating; on the contrary, it was an extension of my art, it showed me new ways, while using the same method."[1]

—Sonia Delaunay

FIG. 1. *Rythme Coloré.* France, 1946. Oil on canvas. Private collection

PREVIOUS PAGE: Design 890f: fabric samples. France, 1929. Produced by Metz & Co, 1938. Printed silk crêpe de chine. Private Collection

Sonia Delaunay was born in 1885 as Sarah Stern to a Jewish laborer's family in Gradizhsk, a village near Odessa, Ukraine.[2] At the age of five, she was adopted by her maternal uncle, Henri Terk, a wealthy lawyer in St. Petersburg. From then on her name was Sonia Terk. She received a Russian bourgeois education in this Jewish intellectual milieu, with governesses who taught her French, English, and German. She was an intelligent pupil, good at mathematics and philosophy. But her greatest interests were art and poetry. Her drawing teacher recognized her talent and advised her adopted parents to send her abroad for further studies. In 1903, Sonia went to Karlsruhe, Germany, to attend the art academy, where she became interested in French Impressionism. Two years after her arrival in Karlsruhe, she went to Paris, a self-confident young woman, zealous and aware of her potential — characteristics she would show all her long and adventurous life (FIG. 2).

Sonia followed courses at the Académie de la Palette, had her own studio, and led a busy social life with other art students and fellow Russian immigrants. Her uncle and aunt wanted her to return to St. Petersburg to marry and establish a family, but Sonia was determined to stay in Paris. With her art dealer and good friend Wilhelm Uhde, she decided to make a marriage of convenience. Through him she gained access to the latest developments in art and new art circles. And in 1907, a year before her marriage to Uhde, she met Robert Delaunay (1885–1941), an ambitious painter of the same age as Sonia.

As soon as they met, Sonia and Robert started intense discussions about the future of art. Robert was interested in the physics of perception, inspired by the French chemist Michel-Eugène Chevreul, author of the seminal 1839 work *De la loi du contraste simultané des couleurs et de l'assortiment des objets colorés…* [*The Principles of Harmony and Contrast of Colors…*] (FIG. 3). Robert studied the effects of light and color and formulated his own theory, which he called Simultaneism. He was interested in using color to paint pure light, and using color contrasts to instill dynamism and rhythm into a painting. While Sonia greatly admired Robert's theoretical statements and studies, she herself tended to work intuitively. He in turn was impressed by Sonia's powerful use of color, which he termed "atavistic," referring to her Ukrainian background (FIG. 1). Although they had very different personalities, they both had a strong spiritual affinity in their artistic aspirations. In the following years, their art strongly resembled each other's, sometimes seeming interchangeable. By 1909, the pair had fallen in love, and in the spring of 1910, Sonia asked Uhde for a divorce; in November of that year, already seven months pregnant, she married Delaunay.

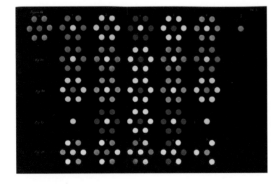

FIG. 2. *Autoportrait no. 962* (self-portrait for the Stockholm catalogue). France, 1916. Encaustic on paper. Private collection

FIRST TEXTILE ART OBJECTS

In 1909, Sonia took up embroidery, which she likely first learned as part of an upper-class Russian girl's education. What would seem at first sight to be a traditionally female occupation would prove to be an essential step in her development. Embroidery became a means to break loose from the academic tradition of line structure dominating color, allowing her to apply color directly to the ground. Moreover, it was a prelude to her fashion and fabric designs (FIG. 4); the same held true for the equally "womanly" skill of patchwork. Whereas embroidered "paintings" were still autonomous works of art, a piece of patchwork is made for household use. In 1911, Sonia made a patchwork quilt for her newborn son Charles. The technique was traditional, but the effect was extremely modern. The pieces of cloth were worked into an abstract pattern, the bold color contrasts seemingly breaking through its surface. She used the same technique on interior furnishing, such as cushions and lampshades, and for decorating book covers.

In 1913, Sonia created her first dress, the *robe simultanée*, or "simultaneous dress." As with the blanket, she had sewn patches of cloth onto the dress, and even added a few pieces of fur. She wore this creation when Robert and she went to the Thursday-evening dances at the Bal Bullier. The dress was also a statement in the direction of the Italian Futurists, who had also entered the field of fashion. The Futurists' eccentric garments were intended to *épater la bourgeoisie*, or shock the establishment. Robert, the poet Blaise Cendrars, and other friends also used to dress in colorful, simultaneity-style attire for these events. Were the Delaunays inspired by the Futurists? The latter liked to think so; Cendrars denied it.[3] In any case, both parties tried to modernize fashion and the daily costume of men and women.

FIG. 3. *De la loi du contraste simultané des couleurs, et de l'assortiment des objets colorés, considéré d'après cette loi... (The Principles of Harmony and Contrast of Colors and Their Application to the Arts...).* Written by Michel Eugène Chevreul (French, 1786–1889). Published by Imprimerie Nationale. France, 1889. Leather, paper, ink, color engraving. Smithsonian Institution Libraries, QND1280.C52 1889

FIG. 4. Model no. 200, *"Feuilles d'automne"* **(Autumn Leaves) panel made from parts of a coat.** France, 1924. Wool embroidery on cotton canvas. Les Arts Décoratifs, Paris, UF 65-10-8

IBERIAN INTERLUDE: CASA SONIA

The Delaunay family was on holiday in the Basque
country in August 1914 when the news reached them that
Germany had declared war on France. Deciding
to stay in Spain, they would stay away for more than six
years, alternating between homes in Spain and
Portugal.[4] The colors, light, sun, and the Portuguese
countryside inspired the couple to produce a great
deal of work, including a series of gouaches of *costumes
simultanés* inspired by the folk clothing worn by women
for festive country dances and for the Spanish flamenco.
At the beginning of 1917, they returned to Spain and
city life. While in Barcelona, they received news of the
Russian Revolution, which resulted in Sonia's family
in St. Petersburg losing all of its property. Sonia lost the
revenues earned from those properties—the Delaunays'
principal source of income at the time. They decided
to go to Madrid, where an increasing number of people
from Paris's international art and culture world were
staying. The Delaunays devised a plan to exploit Sonia's
Simultaneist clothing and interior decorations by
starting up their own business, Casa Sonia. This marked
an important step in Sonia Delaunay's development,
when she ceased to be an independent artist and
joined the world of fashion, dominated by the rules of
commerce, production, and consumer preference.

Once in Madrid, Sonia got in touch with Sergei
Diaghilev, the leader of the Ballets Russes, who had
been in Spain with his company for a number of years
and arrived in Madrid in 1917. Diaghilev introduced
the Delaunays to the Madrid elite as well as to Spanish
financiers. In 1918, he commissioned them to make
designs for his ballet *Cléopâtre*; Robert designed the
stage sets and Sonia the costumes. It was Cleopatra's
dress in particular, a further development of the
robe simultanée, which met with the greatest acclaim.
The premiere in London on September 5, 1918, was
enthusiastically received by the critics. Sonia became
a household name in Madrid, Casa Sonia was a
success, and she considered opening branches in
Bilbao, Barcelona, San Sebastian, and even New York.
In 1920, Sonia went to size up the situation in Paris.

FIG. 5. *Robe poème* (Dress-
poem) no. 688. France,
1922. Watercolor, gouache
and pencil on paper. Museum
of Modern Art, New York
303.1980. Image © The Museum
of Modern Art/Licensed by
SCALA/Art Resource, New York

FIG. 6. *Pyjama for Tristan
Tzara.* France, 1923.
Watercolor and pencil on
paper. Museum of Modern Art,
New York 30.1978. Image
© The Museum of Modern Art/
Licensed by SCALA/Art
Resource, New York

FIG. 7. *Robe-poème pour
Tzara.* France, 1923.
Watercolor on paper.
Private collection

RETURN TO PARIS: THE ROBES POÈMES

Back in Paris, Sonia was elated by the city's effervescent optimism and very taken with the Dadaists. Robert and Sonia could not resist the temptation to settle again in their former city. They found themselves a large apartment on the fifth floor of 19, boulevard Malesherbes, an ideal place to work as well as entertain friends and relatives. Sonia transformed the rooms into a three-dimensional collage using her own Simultaneist decorations with additions from poet friends and other guests. Sonia enjoyed working with other artists, especially poets. Her feeling was that her art, whether it was a painting, dress, or whatever, was a form of poetry. With new Dada friends came new projects. Sonia embroidered a poem that Philippe Soupault had dedicated to her on a light gray silk curtain using red and black silks. It became known as the *rideau poème* (curtain poem), and on special occasions, she wore it as an evening cape. In 1922, she made several robes poèmes, based on works provided by Tristan Tzara, Joseph Delteil, and others. These "poems in motion" were worn by audacious young women at places "where you were meant to be seen."[5] (FIGS. 5–9)

Sonia designed costumes for several Dada evenings and other occasions, such as Tzara's absurd play *Le Coeur à Gaz* (1923). When working on this type of assignment, she took her costume experiments a step further. For a dance improvisation to music by composer Francis Poulenc called *Mouvement Perpétuel*, the Rumanian dancer Lizica Codreanu performed in a Sonia Delaunay suit consisting of colored cardboard discs around her neck, waist, and wrists, which she moved and turned while dancing — Simultaneist choreography. A step beyond what could be achieved on paper or canvas, the experiment was a continuation of Sonia's studies of the color and rhythm of Portuguese and Spanish dance, and was related to developments in Constructivist theatre in Russia and with the Bauhaus.[6]

FIG. 8. *Robe poème
no. 1329.* France, 1923.
Watercolor, gouache and
pencil on paper. Museum
of Modern Art, New York
301.1980. Image © The Museum
of Modern Art/Licensed by
SCALA/Art Resource, New York

FIG. 9. *Robe poème no. 1328.*
France, 1923. Watercolor,
gouache and pencil on
paper. Museum of Modern Art,
New York 304.1980. Image
© The Museum of Modern
Art/Licensed by SCALA/Art
Resource, New York

GIRAU

SONIA
DELAU
NAY
SIMULTANE

HEIM
FURS

LEFRT-MAROQUINERIE

SONIA DELAUNAY

GUEVREKIAN - ARCHITECTE

FASHION AND FABRIC DESIGNER

**FIG. 10. Boutique Simultané,
René Herbst, *Devantures,
vitrines, installations
de magasins à l'exposition
internationale des arts
décoratifs*, Paris, France,
1925, plate 18.** Smithsonian
Institution Libraries. FNA6225.H42

LA MAISON DELAUNAY
AND THE ATELIER SIMULTANÉ

Sonia was still toying with the idea of a renewed Casa
Sonia. Money had to be earned, and it had become
clear that it would not come from the sales of Robert's
paintings. Sonia's great success with her costumes
and fashion presentations at Dada evenings and benefit
parties seemed to indicate that there was a market
for her fashion in Paris. In March 1925 Sonia registered
with the Board of Trade using the trade name "Sonia"
and the trademark "Simultané."[7] Funded by a few loans,
she was able to start her Maison Delaunay in her newly
decorated apartment.[8]

In July 1925 came Sonia's great breakthrough at
the *Exposition des Arts Décoratifs et Industriels Modernes*
in Paris. This exhibition was a celebration of Paris as
a world capital of art and luxury, and Sonia's designs
fit this image. She had been given the chance to
present herself by Jacques Heim of the renowned fur
and fashion house Heim. He had arranged for her
to decorate the presentation room, called *la Boutique
Simultané*, and design fur coats using her appliqué
technique (FIG. 10). She also showed a collection of coats,
jackets, bags, shoes, scarves, and wraps boasting
embroidered geometric patterns, which she had made
by Russian embroiderers and seamstresses, refugees
from Bolshevism who had lost their bourgeois clientèle
as a result of the Revolution and sought refuge in
Paris.[9] (FIGS. 11–13) Sonia's work was unanimously praised
in the press, and many orders poured in from the likes
of the wives of architects Walter Gropius, Marcel Breuer,
and Erich Mendelsohn, celebrities such as the American
film star Gloria Swanson (FIG. 15), Parisian actresses
Paulette Pax, Lucienne Bogaert, Gabrielle Diorzat, Eyre
de Lanux (FIG. 17), and the English writer and avant-
garde muse Nancy Cunard (FIG. 19). Photographs of stars
dressed in Sonia's clothes began to circulate (FIG. 18),

as did a portfolio of silkscreen prints of her paintings,
objects, fashion, and fabrics with texts by Joseph
Delteil, Blaise Cendrars, Philippe Soupault, and Tristan
Tzara. Her costumes for two French films of the period,
Le P'tit Parigot and *Le Vertige,* confirmed Sonia's
reputation as an ultramodern fashion designer (FIG. 16).

Sonia Delaunay did not view her designs as a
devaluation of her art, but rather as an extension of
her field.[10] Her belief fit in well with modernist theories
about the reunification of art and life, achieved
by abandoning the painter's easel and getting closer
to art in everyday life, including advertisements,
architecture, furniture, fashion, fabrics, and household
utensils. Similar ideas could also be found in allied
artistic trends like Futurism, Neo-Plasticism, *de Stijl* and
Constructivism. Usually these experimental designs
were only used by the group that produced them. They
were more statements than designs meant to attract
a larger group of consumers. Sonia set herself apart
from the rest because her designs went commercial.
Robert played a role in the enterprise. He signed the
business agreements, registered design and brand
names, and often dealt with the finances. He designed
a moving fabric display and other forms of presentation
and allowed his studio to be used for photo sessions
(FIG. 14). Moreover, he painted portraits of friends and
acquaintances dressed in Sonia's creations. The
affinity between the producer of luxury consumer goods
and the avant-garde painter is interesting, as they
were instrumental to each other, so much so that neither
could be seen as a separate entity. Sonia's fashion, and
all the publicity surrounding it, promoted Simultaneism;
on the other hand, Simultaneism provided Sonia's
fashion with artistic status, which appealed to a
specific clientele. The binding factor was the image

FIG. 11. Scarf, Tissu simultané (Simultaneous textile) no. 70. Printed by Ferret. France, 1924. Block-printed silk crêpe de chine. Les Arts Décoratifs, Paris, 40402

FIG. 12. Scarf. France, 1924–25. Wool reverse appliqué. Musée de l'Impression sur Étoffes, Mulhouse, 980.634.1

FIG. 13. Scarf. France, 1924–25. Woven wool. Musée de l'Impression sur Étoffes, Mulhouse, 980.638.1

of the modern woman.[11] But despite all the publicity, not many people actually wore Sonia's clothes. The Parisian women who could afford it opted mainly for the sophisticated elegance of couturiers like Chanel, Lanvin, or Patou.[12]

Despite the fact that Sonia gave her business her all, Maison Delaunay lacked a strong business model. Manager and financial director of Maison Delaunay from 1926–29 was Jean Coutrot, a business contact of Robert's. Sonia does not mention Coutrot in her memoirs; however, there is interesting information in Coutrot's files about the business side of Maison Delaunay.[13] The fabrics—not fashion—were of primary financial importance. Sonia sold fabric designs to manufacturers in France and abroad including America. The fashion fabrics produced by Maison Delaunay from a selection of the best designs sold very successfully to Parisian *maisons de couture* and firms that exported them abroad, and they formed the foundation of the enterprise. The fashion workshop itself, however, with its eight to ten employees, was unprofitable, and its main purpose, according to Coutrot, was to serve as advertisement for the fabrics. But he was sure it had potential and suggested several improvements. As Sonia's clientele comprised too many artists, journalists, and others who paid little

FIG. 14. Sonia Delaunay (at right) and two models in Robert Delaunay's studio, 1924. Bibliothèque Nationale de France, Paris

or nothing for the goods, Coutrot suggested they employ a professional sales assistant with a network of clients. Because Maison Delaunay lacked a proper storefront, he proposed to arrange sales outlets at Hermès and other established fashion houses or department stores. Lastly, he urged her to keep a closer eye on the finances and cut costs.

Coutrot's advice didn't appeal to Sonia, who was frightened her creations would be vulgarized and that she would lose her independence. But she must have been aware that Coutrot was right, as correspondence from 1929 reveals that she approached another advisor with a sort of business plan which mentioned the necessity of scaling up, injecting new capital, and improving customer relations.[14]

After the Wall Street stock-market crash in October 1929, orders stopped coming in, and soon the firm's financial problems were such that Sonia closed down her ailing Maison. She described it afterwards as a great relief. The financial crisis had saved her, she wrote. No more worries about employees, wages, customers, publicity. But this is not the complete story. Under the flag of her trademark, since 1929 called Tissus Delaunay, Sonia continued to create and sell fabric designs.

FIG. 15. Coat made for Gloria Swanson. France, 1923–24. Wool embroidery on cotton canvas. Private collection

FIG. 16. Still photo from the film *Le P'tit Parigot*. Written by Paul Cartoux. Directed by René Le Somptier. France, 1926. Collection of Antoine Blanchette

FIG. 17. Eyre de Lanux in Sonia Delaunay coat, ca. 1928. Collection of Antoine Blanchette

FIG. 18. Postcard of two models wearing Sonia Delaunay coats at the Exposition des Arts Décoratifs. Paris, France, 1925. Private collection

FIG. 19. Portrait of Nancy Cunard. France, 1924. China crayon on paper. Courtesy of Barry Friedman and Patricia Pastor

TISSUS DELAUNAY

Since 1923, Sonia Delaunay had been designing
printed fabrics, the so-called "tissus simultanés," as
a logical development from her embroidered or
appliquéd designs for clothing. She used them in her
fashion designs and accessories and sold them to
firms in France or abroad. After the demise of her fashion
house, Sonia became a professional textile designer.
Especially in the early 1930s, Sonia Delaunay carried
on the business as a one-person enterprise. She also
continued to design clothes for a limited clientele,
and designed interiors for well-to-do friends too. The
fabric designs that she had assembled in the previous
years in her design books — the *livres noirs*, or black
books — were still being bought by textile factories in
various countries, and she was still producing many
new designs (FIGS. 24–61).

To cope with the business's administration and
bookkeeping, which she considered an enormous
headache, she started a journal in 1933 — a combined
diary, agenda, and housekeeping book.[15] She
maintained the journal until 1969, and it is a unique
source of information about the daily life of an
indefatigable artist and entrepreneur. It reveals the
creative process of some of her designs, shows her
relations with people who commissioned work from her,
and tells of visits from friends in the Parisian art world.

FIG. DETAILS. 28–61.
FIGS. 24–61, P56–85.

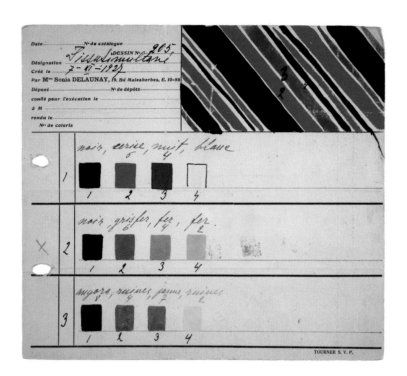

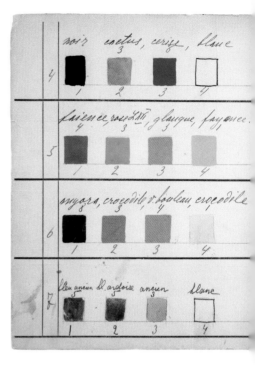

METZ & CO

When Sonia Delaunay began her journal on February 27, 1933, her first note concerned a commission by the Amsterdam firm of Metz & Co. Metz was a relatively small luxury department store selling interior furnishings, applied art products, fabrics, and fashion. Begun as a small business of silk merchants in Amsterdam's Jewish quarter around 1740, Metz became a wholesale company that delivered French silks all over the Netherlands. By the end of the nineteenth century, Metz had opened a shop in the center of Amsterdam. In 1902, it became the first agent of London's Liberty & Co. on the continent. Apart from Arts & Crafts–style fabrics, Metz also sold Liberty's fashion, gifts, and interior decoration. Responsible for this was the visionary and commercially talented director Joseph de Leeuw (1872–1944). In 1918, Metz & Co began exclusive production of objects designed by modern and avant-garde artists and architects. Combined with Liberty fabrics and other products, this made Metz & Co a favorite shop for the elite.[16]

The name Metz occurs frequently in Sonia's journal, as it was one of her most important clients during the 1930s, and a cooperation that lasted into the 1960s. A deep friendship also developed between Sonia and De Leeuw. His son Hendrik de Leeuw (1908–1978) took over the family business after the war until he retired and sold the company to Liberty's in 1973. He continued to commission designs from Sonia, and the De Leeuw family remained close friends of hers until her death in 1979.

Joseph de Leeuw first encountered Sonia Delaunay and saw her fabric designs at the 1925 international exhibition in Paris,[17] and the first Metz orders date from that year.[18] An ambitious entrepreneur always in search of new ideas and articles, De Leeuw was neither greatly impressed by Dutch textile design nor particularly interested in work from abroad, and he felt that Sonia's work was just what he needed to modernize the Metz collection. In the 1920s, the orders were ready-made products from Maison Delaunay; from 1930 onwards, Metz bought designs from Sonia and produced them on its own.

Altogether, Sonia Delaunay created over two thousand different designs. Through the years, Metz bought over two hundred of them, and continued

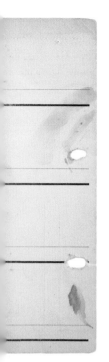

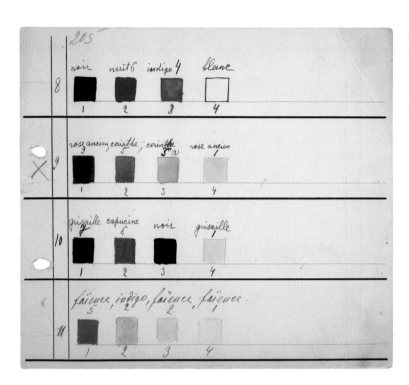

FIG. 20. Tissu simultané no. 205: design cards. France, 1927. Fabric produced by Metz & Co, 1934. Gouache, ink, and pencil on paper. Private collection

to produce and sell them until the mid-1960s. A considerable quantity of these designs and samples has been preserved, in particular the prewar fashion fabrics and the "fabric books," similar to Sonia's livres noirs, kept by Metz as records of their textile production. They provide a great deal of information over the years until 1940 (FIG. 21), and, combined with Sonia's journal and her livres noirs, it is possible to reconstruct her working method and the business and personal relations between her and Joseph and Hendrik de Leeuw and Metz.

In early 1933, when Sonia Delaunay began keeping records in her journal, she was busy producing, among other things, interior and fashion fabrics for Metz. The word "producing" is appropriate, since what Sonia did comprised far more than simply drawing a design. In the days of Maison Delaunay, she had supervised the printing of textiles herself and maintained connections with several textile production companies. The entire process — design, discussions with engravers and printers, assessing proofs, sending samples — was overseen by her. This level of quality control proved invaluable to De Leeuw, a client in a distant city. He also made frequent trips to Paris to discuss production details with Sonia.

Much time went into the selection of designs. Sonia's notes give the impression that De Leeuw paid far more attention to this than did other clients. Patterns were enlarged or made smaller, colors were adapted, sometimes for technical reasons. It says much about Sonia's confidence in De Leeuw's judgment and the strength of their friendship that she permitted such alterations to her designs. Metz employed many different fabric printers, in Britain, France, Germany, and Japan. Most of the textiles were luxury fabrics, printed by hand on high-quality material. A design would be printed in several color combinations and on two or more types of fabric. Usually one design was printed on a length of no more than thirty meters, and further orders could be repeated. Sonia's fashion fabrics were mostly hand-printed silks, cotton, or rayon.

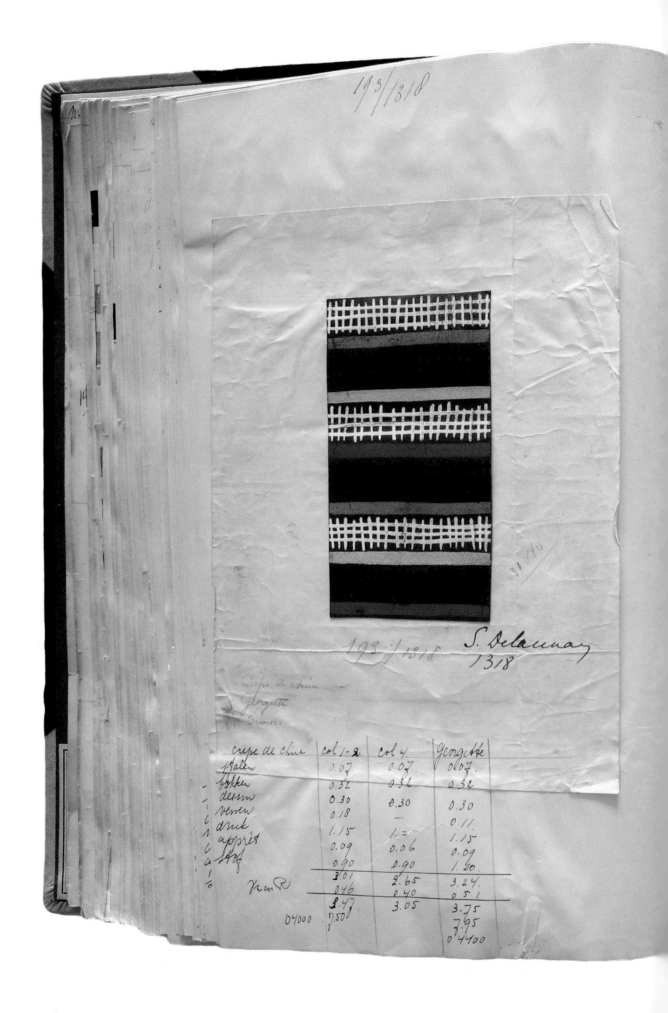

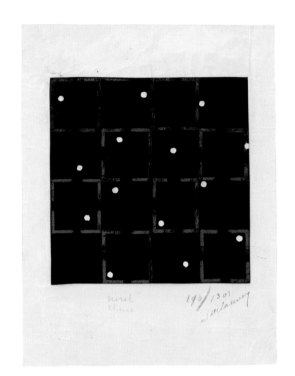

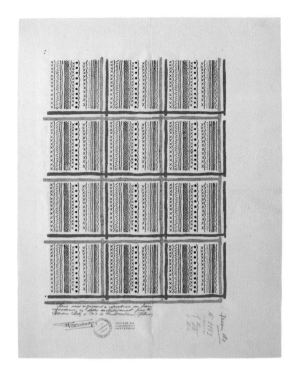

PREVIOUS PAGE:
FIG. 21. Metz & Co fabric book with Design 1318.
France, 1934. Gouache, ink, and pencil on paper with fabric swatches.
Private collection

FIG. 22. *Design 1303.*
France, 1934. Produced by Metz & Co. Gouache, ink, and pencil on paper.
Private collection

FIG. 23. Design 1153: master print, fabric samples.
France, 1932. Produced by Metz & Co, 1933. Printed by Petitdidier. Colorprint, pencil, and ink on paper; printed silk. Private collection

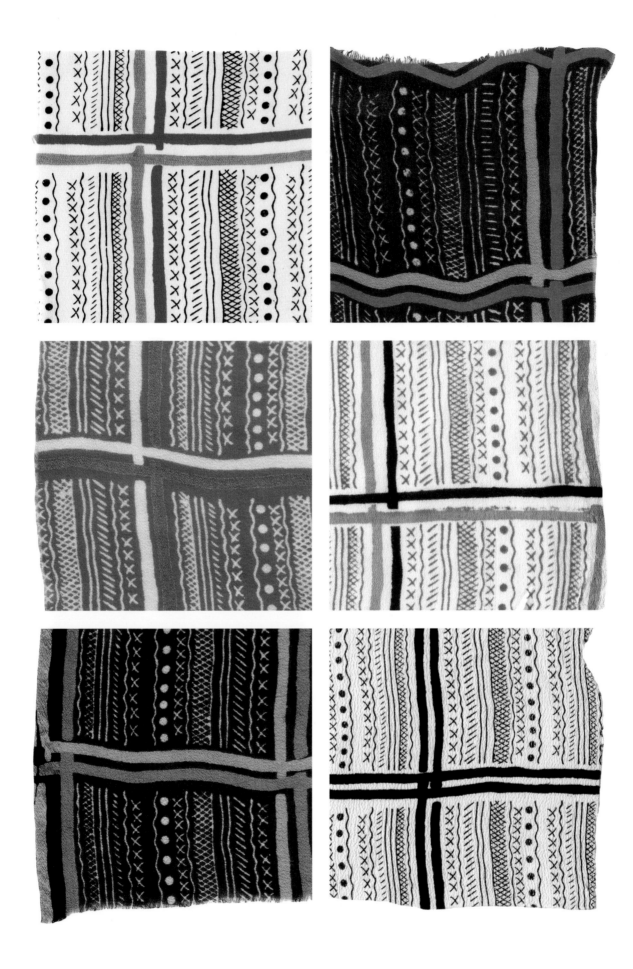

FIG. DETAILS. 62–73.
FIGS. 62–73, P86–101.

THE DESIGNS

Sonia's early Paris fashion designs were dominated by huge geometric patterns (FIGS. 24–61). These patterns of contrasting areas of color arose at the same time as the design for the dress. The fabric designs, intended originally for her own fashion garments, turned out to be works in their own right, developing a life of their own, with their own use of color and visual language. This development can be partly explained if we consider that Sonia was dependent upon clients and the changing world of fashion. During the 1930s, fashion became less outrageous and more restful than in the previous decade. Sonia's patterns also grew smaller and to a certain extent more conventional. On the other hand, she grew more practiced at designing fabrics, acquiring a greater feel for the supple movement of materials when worn and for the repetitive nature of a fabric design. It was by exploiting the possibilities and limitations inherent in fabric design that Sonia created arresting patterns (FIG. 23).

Sonia's textile designs reveal a repertoire of forms that appear nowhere in her other art. Her patterns are composed of simple stripes, small strokes, crosses, and dots. Crosses turn into flowers, stripes form check patterns, dots become blocks, in a myriad of combinations. Many of her designs are related to each other in their variations. If you look at her patterns over the years, you discover something like family likenesses. Omissions or irregularities in the repeat patterns add vigor (FIG. 22). This vitality is increased by the individual lines, which form the essential "signature" of an artist. Sonia's designs give the impression of great spontaneity, and the fabrics reflect this lighthearted, almost nonchalant tone. This effect is difficult to attain when transposed to a textile because of the technical processes. The printer has to imitate the paint stroke and the irregularity of hand-drawn lines

in the wood or linoleum printing blocks or metal rollers used to print into the fabric. It is clear from one of the notes on a proof print that Sonia aimed at this spontaneous effect: *"Raies moins rigides, légèrement ondulantes"* ("stripes less rigid, lightly wavy").[19]

The fabrics Sonia made for Metz provide a representative cross-section of her textile designs. We find all types of design in them: checks, blocks, stripes, circles (far fewer in her textile designs than in her other work), abstract shapes, and, of course, the flowers. In general, these latter designs are not what one immediately associates with Sonia Delaunay. However, she made a large number of floral designs ranging from single flower motifs to huge, roughly drawn blooms. Flowers had already appeared in her fashion designs and interior decorations in Spain (ca. 1918–20). In any case, they were amply represented in the Metz collection (FIGS. 62–73). At times they recall folk art and remind us of Sonia's Russian background, while others resemble the stylized idiom of Art Deco.

Great consideration went into Sonia's palette. She numbered all of her colors and gave them verbal

descriptions, such as "cactus green" and "angora gray" (FIG. 20). She sometimes used startling colors in her textiles but was not always out after arresting contrasts.[20] She had an extensive palette from which she created her color combinations ("coloris"). She used fresh, clear mixtures such as red, green, blue, black, or white, which form the hallmark of her oeuvre. But she also had subtler combinations of delicate pastel hues, or mixed strong colors with soft or somber tones.

The idea of Simultaneism became less prominent in her textile designs. Indeed, by the 1930s, the expression "tissus simultanés" was no longer used. Although Sonia was no less aware of the effects of certain color combinations, the visual impact of color contrasts was not her most important theme, as it was in her paintings. The designs, with their range of forms and color, can be seen as an independent part in her total work rather than as an offshoot of her painting.

Although Sonia Delaunay might be best known as a modern painter—an image she herself created—she wholeheartedly admitted the importance and creative inspiration of her textile work. Sonia Delaunay

regarded herself and Robert as visionaries who could sense the changes of their times and translate them into new forms. They reacted to the world around them and thus created innovations.[21] In a 1962 letter to Hendrik de Leeuw, she refers to this, underlining the importance of her textile designs (and showing that modesty was not her strongest characteristic):

"Our position in life and its evolution are important and unique because, parallel to important developments in art, we introduced art into daily life. I started this in 1911, when I created the baby blanket for our son, shown nowadays in art galleries as one of the first abstract paintings. Then the book covers of 1913... the robes simultanées of 1913–14, and later on the fabrics and embroidered coats—they all stand in close relationship to the laws of painting. From 1924 until 1930, this made me well-known in the whole world, especially the United States. This contributed greatly to the comprehension of modern art, which became more accessible and understandable through my fabrics, which for me were exercises in color."[22]

**FIG. 24. Model wearing
Sonia Delaunay coat.**
France, 1923–29. Bibliothèque
Nationale de France, Paris

**FIG.25. Driving caps.
France, 1924–28.** Silk and
wool embroidery on cotton
canvas. Musée de la Mode
de la Ville de Paris, Musée
Galliera, GAL 1971.24.3 A-D

FIG. 26. **Model wearing Sonia Delaunay coat, ca. 1925.** Bibliothèque Nationale de France, Paris

FIG. 27. **Three models wearing Sonia Delaunay coats in the Bois de Boulogne, Paris, ca. 1927.** Bibliothèque Nationale de France, Paris

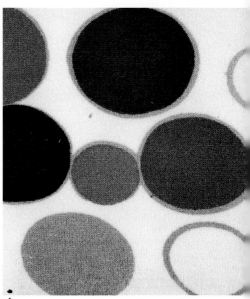

FIG. 28 A–C. Tissu simultané no. 193. France, 1927. Block-printed silk, cotton, wool jersey. Musée de l'Impression sur Étoffes, Mulhouse, 980.554.4, 16, 6

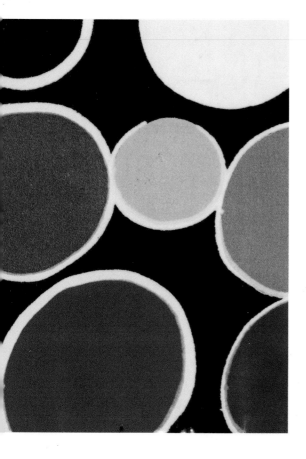

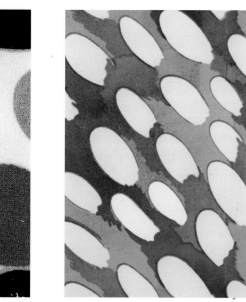

FIG. 29. Tissu simultané no. 923. France, 1929. Block-printed silk crêpe de chine. Musée de l'Impression sur Étoffes, Mulhouse, 980.611.8

FIG. 30. Two models
wearing Sonia Delaunay
beachwear, 1928.
Private collection

FIG. 31A, B. Tissu simultané no. 186. France, 1926. Block-printed cotton.
Musée de l'Impression sur Étoffes, Mulhouse, 980.549.17, 18

FIG. 32. Skirt, Tissu simultané no. 186. France, ca. 1926. Block-printed wool jersey. Musée de l'Impression sur Étoffes, Mulhouse, 980.549.11

FIG. 33. Scarf, Tissu simultané no. 186. France, 1926. Block-printed silk. Private collection

FIG. 34. Projet de tissu simultané (Design for Simultaneous Textile) no. 186. Blocks carved by Ferret. France, 1926. Watercolor on paper. Les Arts Décoratifs, Paris, 40406

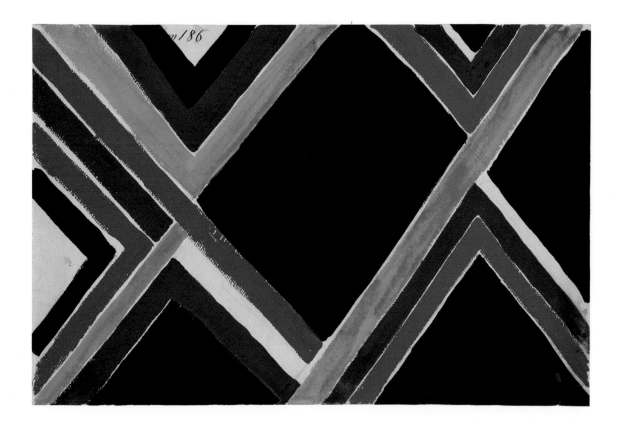

FIG. 35. Model wearing Sonia Delaunay swimsuit, 1929. Photographed by Luigi Diaz for Presse Paris. Bibliothèque Nationale de France

FIG. 37. Bathing suit. France, ca. 1928. Knitted wool. Musée de la Mode de la Ville de Paris, Musée Galliera, GAL 1971.24.7

FIG. 36. Bathing suit (tunic). France, 1924–25. Silk embroidery on wool jersey. Musée de l'Impression sur Étoffes, Mulhouse, 980.629.1

FIG. 38. Bathing suit (tunic and shorts), Tissu simultané no. 205. France, 1927. Block-printed cotton. Musée de l'Impression sur Étoffes, Mulhouse, 980.621.1,2

FIGS. 39A, B. Hat and scarf.
France, 1923. Block-
printed cotton, silk tassels.
Musée de l'Impression sur
Étoffes, Mulhouse, 980.620.1,2

**FIGS. 40A, B. Tissue simultané
no. 205.** France, 1927. Block-
printed on cotton velveteen,
cotton. Musée de l'Impression sur
Étoffes, Mulhouse, 980.563.25

FIG. 41. *Projet de tissu simultané.* Blocks carved by Ferret. France, 1927. Watercolor on paper. Les Arts Décoratifs, Paris, 40411

FIG. 42. **Tissu simultané no. 204.** Printed by Ferret. France, 1927. Block-printed silk crêpe de chine. Les Arts Décoratifs, Paris, 40412 A-B

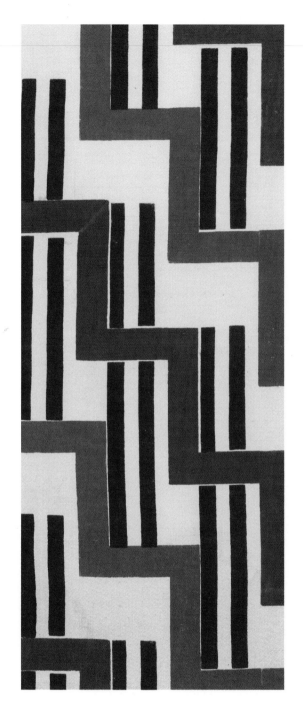

FIG. 43. Two models in Sonia Delaunay's boulevard Malesherbes studio, 1925. Photographed by Germaine Krull. Bibliothèque Nationale de France, Paris

FIG. 44. Tissu simultané no. 166. France, 1926. Block-printed cotton. Musée de l'Impression sur Étoffes, Mulhouse, 980.503.4

FIG. 45. Tissu simultané no. 46. France, 1924. Block-printed cotton. Musée de l'Impression sur Étoffes, Mulhouse, 980.501.2

FIG. 46. Skirt panel, Tissu simultané no. 11. France, 1924. Block-printed silk crêpe de chine. Musée de l'Impression sur Étoffes, Mulhouse, 980.518.3

FIG. 47. Model wearing Sonia Delaunay dress, ca. 1927. Bibliothèque Nationale de France, Paris

FIG. 48. Shawl. France,
1925–30. Knitted wool.
Les Arts Décoratifs, Paris, 47694

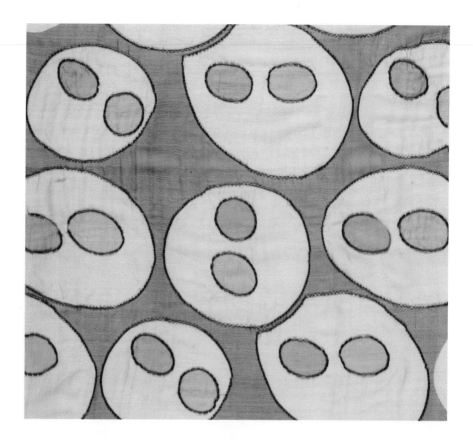

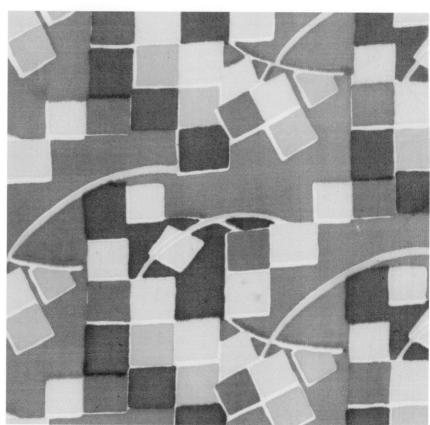

FIG. 49. Tissu simultané no. 7. France, 1924–25. Block-printed silk chiffon, silk embroidery, glass beads. Musée de l'Impression sur Étoffes, Mulhouse, 980.516.5

FIG. 50. Tissu simultané no. 266. France, 1928. Block-printed silk. Musée de l'Impression sur Étoffes, Mulhouse, 980.567.5

FIGS. 51A, B. Tissu simultané no. 214. France, 1928. Block-printed silk velvet, silk crêpe de chine. Musée de l'Impression sur Étoffes, Mulhouse, 980.563BIS.5, 8

FIGS. 52A, B. Tissu simultané no. 145. France, 1926. Block-printed silk crêpe de chine. Musée de l'Impression sur Étoffes, Mulhouse, 980.539.2, 4

FIG. 53. Projet de tissu simultané no. 30. France, 1924. Watercolor on paper. Les Arts Décoratifs, Paris, 40395

FIG. 54. Composition abstracte diagonale (Abstract Diagonal Composition) no. 1733. France, 1925. Gouache on paper. Private collection

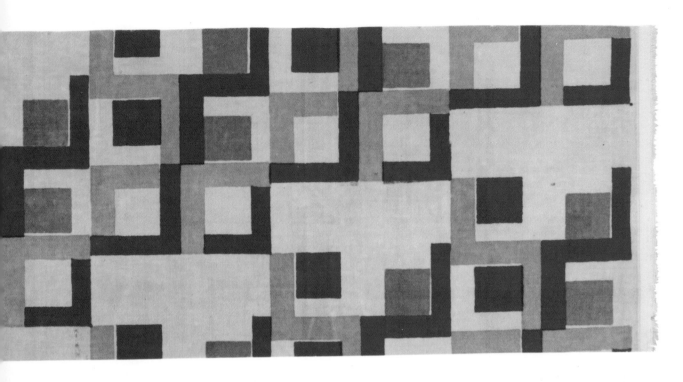

FIG. 55. Tissu simultané.
France, 1924–25. Block-
printed cotton velveteen.
Musée de l'Impression sur
Étoffes, Mulhouse, 980.614.2

FIG. 56. Tissu simultané.
France, 1924–25. Block-
printed cotton velveteen.
Musée de l'Impression sur Étoffes,
Mulhouse, 980.507.1

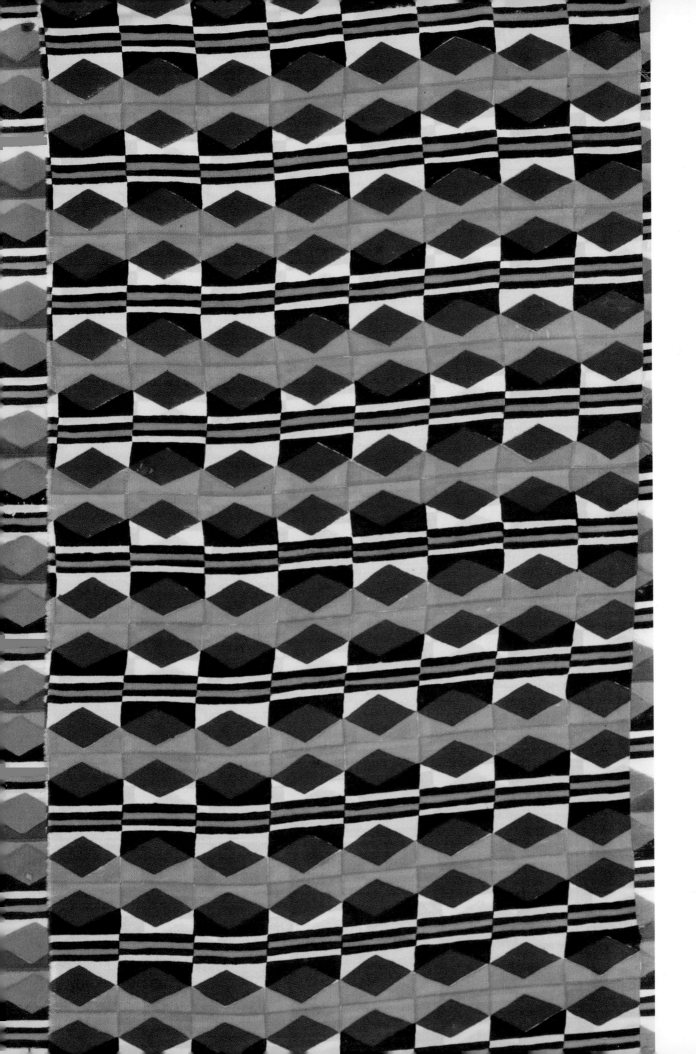

**FIG. 57. Tissu simultané
fabric samples.** France,
1926. Block-printed silk crêpe
de chine. Musée de l'Impression
sur Étoffes, Mulhouse, 980.513.1-4

**FIG. 58. *Projet de tissu
simultané no. 25.*** France,
1924. Watercolor on paper.
Les Arts Décoratifs, Paris, 40394

FIG. 59. Scarf, Tissu simultané no. 14. France, 1924–25. Block-printed cotton. Musée de l'Impression sur Étoffes, Mulhouse, 980.619.1

FIG. 60. Projet de tissu simultané no. 33. France, 1924. Watercolor on paper. Les Arts Décoratifs, Paris, 40396

FIG. 61. Tissu simultané. France, ca. 1924. Block-printed silk crêpe de chine. Musée de l'Impression sur Étoffes, Mulhouse, 980.514.1

FIG. 62. Design 1324: Fabric sample, textile design, and master print. France, 1934. Produced by Metz & Co. Printed silk; gouache and pencil on paper; colorprint, pencil, and ink on paper. Private collection

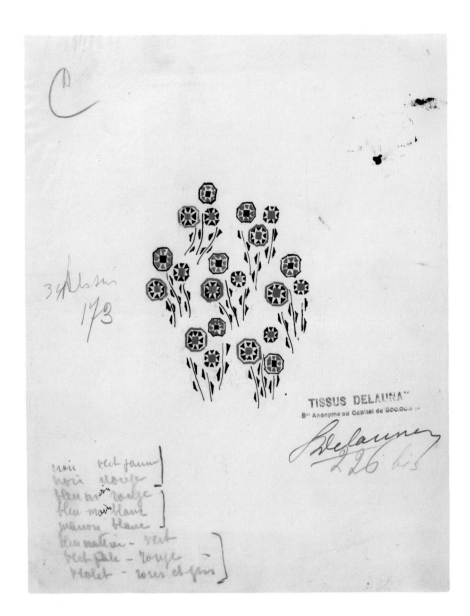

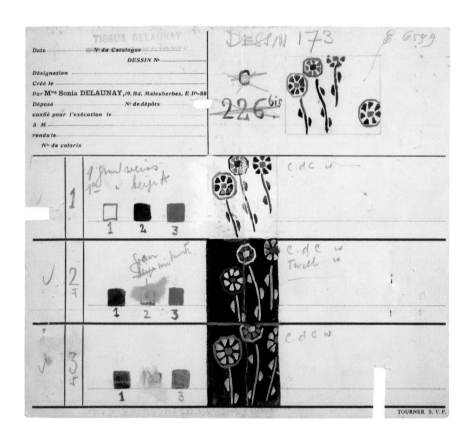

FIGS. 63A–E. Design 226bis: textile design, fabric samples, design cards. France, 1928. Produced by Metz & Co, 1930. Gouache, ink, and pencil on paper; printed silk. Private collection

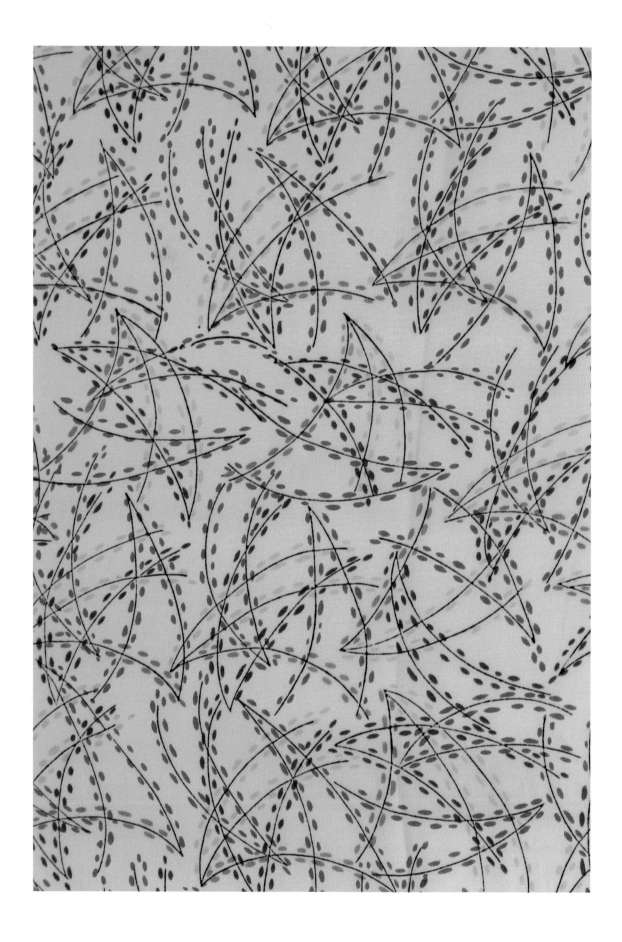

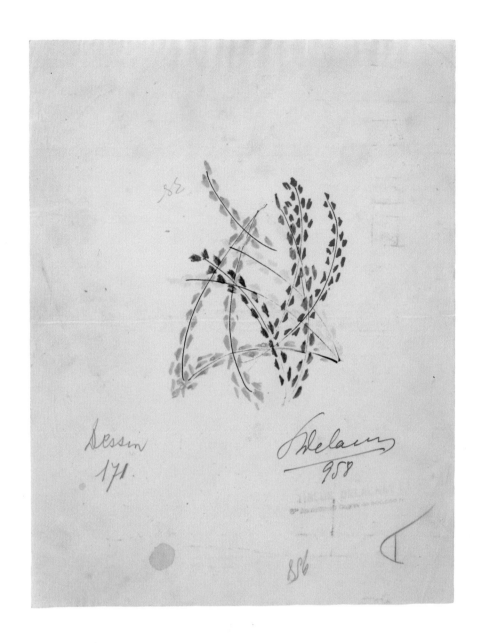

**FIGS. 64A, B. Design 958:
fabric sample, textile
design.** France, 1929.
Produced by Metz & Co,
1930. Printed silk crêpe
de chine; gouache, ink,
and pencil on paper.
Private collection

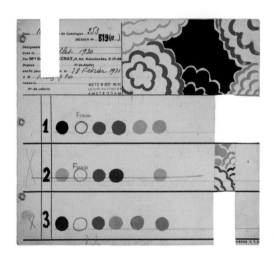

FIGS. 65A–D. Design 253: textile design, collage, design card, fabric sample. France, 1928–30. Produced by Metz & Co, 1931. Gouache, ink, and pencil on paper; collage of gouache on tracing paper, lined; gouache, ink and pencil on paper; printed cotton mousseline. Private collection

FIG. 66. *Design 1488.*
France, 1934–36. Gouache
on paper. Private collection

FIG. 67. *Design 1489.*
France, 1934–36. Gouache
on paper. Private collection

FIG. 68. *Design 1486.*
France, 1934–36. Gouache
on paper. Private collection

FIG. 69. *Design 1487.*
France, 1934–36. Gouache
on paper. Private collection

FIG. 70. *Design 1490.*
France, 1934–36. Gouache
and pencil on paper.
Private collection

FIG. 71. *Design 1492,*
1492bis. France, 1934–36.
Gouache on paper.
Private collection

FIG. 72. *Design 1493.*
France, 1934–36. Gouache
on paper. Private collection

FIG. 73. *Design 1494.*
France, 1934–36. Gouache
on paper. Private collection

NOTES

1   Sonia Delaunay, *Nous irons jusqu'au soleil*,
    Paris 1979, p. 96.

PAGE 25

2   This essay is partly based on several articles I wrote on
    Sonia Delaunay between 1992 and 2008, which were
    originally translated into English by Wendie Shaffer
    and Kate Williams.

    Sonia Delaunay, Metz est venu (Amsterdam: Stedelijk
    Museum, 1992); *Sonia Delaunay, Tecidos Simultâneos*
    (Porto: Museu Soares dos Reis, 2001–2); "Sonia
    Delaunay, Fashion and Fabric Designer," in
    Simultanke, Ustvarjalni Svet Sonie Delaunay (Ljubljana:
    Mednarodni graficni likovni center, 2005): 29–48;
    "Sonia Delaunays Stoffenentwürfe für Metz & Co" in
    Sonia Delaunays Welt der Kunst (Kunsthalle Bielefeld,
    2008–9: 193–204.

PAGE 26

3   G. Lista, "La mode futuriste," in *Europe 1900–1939,
    Quand l'art habillait le vêtement* (Paris, 1997)
    pp. 22–42, p. 30. See also R. Stern, *Against Fashion,
    Clothing as Art 1850–1930* (Cambridge, MA, and
    London, 2004): 65.

PAGE 28

4   For the Delaunays' stay in Spain and Portugal, see
    Robert i Sonia Delaunay, exh. cat. (Barcelona: Picasso
    Museum, 2000), and *Sonia Delaunay Tecidos
    Simultâneos.*

PAGE 29

5   G. Bernier and M. Schneider-Maunoury,
    Robert et Sonia Delaunay. Naissance de l'art abstrait
    (Paris, 1995): 192.

6   S. Buckberrough, *Sonia Delaunay. A Retrospective*
    (Buffalo, 1980): 61.

PAGE 33

7   V. Guillaume, "Sonia und Tissus Delaunay.
    Sonia Delaunay als Unternehmerin," in *Robert
    Delaunay Sonia Delaunay, das Centre Pompidou zu
    Gast in Hamburg,* Hamburger Kunsthalle 1999,
    pp. 30–37, p.33.

8   Maison Delaunay indicates Sonia's house of fashion
    and fabric. This is not a shop in the true sense, with a
    display in a shop window like the Boutique Silmultané
    at the 1925 Paris exposition. (If you were interested
    in a Maison Delaunay dress, you could go to the
    Delaunay apartment by appointment.) Atelier
    Simultané is the studio of Maison Delaunay, where
    Sonia designed her fashion and fabrics and the
    workshop where her seamstresses worked until 1930.

9   For more about these Russian émigrés, see:
    V. Guillaume, *"Les artistes russes à Paris et la mode,"* in
    Europe 1910-1939, Quand l'art habillait le vêtement
    (Paris: Palais Galliéra): 82–92.

10 Annette Malochet, who has analyzed Sonia's *livres
    noirs* (ca. 1924–34), reveals how technically detailed
    fabric designs, fashion sketches, and free color
    designs *(recherches)* alternated with one another,
    in constant interaction. A. Malochet, "L'atelier
    Simultanée de Sonia Delaunay," in *Sonia Delaunay.
    L'Atelier Simultanée 1923-1934. Aquarelles et gouaches,*
    exh. cat. (Musée de Lodève, 2002–3): 25–45.

PAGE 35

11 T. Gronberg, "Sonia Delaunay's Simultaneous
    Fashions and the Modern Woman," in W. Chadwick,
    T. True Latimer (ed.), *The Modern Woman Revisited.
    Paris Between the Wars* (New Brunswick, NJ, and
    London, 2003): 109–23.

12 M. Schneider-Maunoury, "Sonia Delaunay.
    The Clothing of Modernity," in *Art/Fashion*
    (New York: Guggenheim Museum, 1996): 65.

13 V. Guillaume, pp. 86–93.

PAGE 37

14 Documentation Delaunay, box Affaires, projets (n.d.),
    correspondance with Mme Delafoye. Centre Georges
    Pompidou, Bibliothèque Kandinsky.

PAGE 42

15 The Journal (1933–69) is in the Bibliothèque
    Nationale in Paris.

PAGE 44

16 In *Metz & Co, de creatieve jaren* (Rotterdam, 1995),
    I describe the history of Metz & Co and the patronage
    of its directors. In 2000, I published my doctoral thesis
    about the avant-garde and commerce, an epilogue
    essay to the former publication.

17 As told by the De Leeuw family.

18 In Metz's administration dealing with French
    creditors, Sonia's name appears in 1925/6.
    "Fransche crediteuren," in Metz archive,
    Amsterdam City Archives.

PAGE 50

19 Sometimes the printing blocks were made in Sonia's
    workshop, but she usually had them produced by
    Ferret in Saint-Denis, near Paris.

20 Letter from Sonia Delaunay dated 2 June 1926,
    printed in *Sonia Delaunay*, exh. cat.
    (Städtisches Kunsthaus Bielefeld, 1958).

PAGE 51

21 "Tapis et Tissus, présenté par S.D.," in: *L'Art
    international* 15 (Paris 1929), as presented
    in V. Guillaume, 'Les artistes russes à Paris et la
    mode," in *Europe 1910-1939, quand l'art habillait
    le vêtement*, p. 97.

22 Attachment (March 20, 1962) to a letter from
    S. Delaunay to H. de Leeuw, March 27, 1962.
    Private collection.

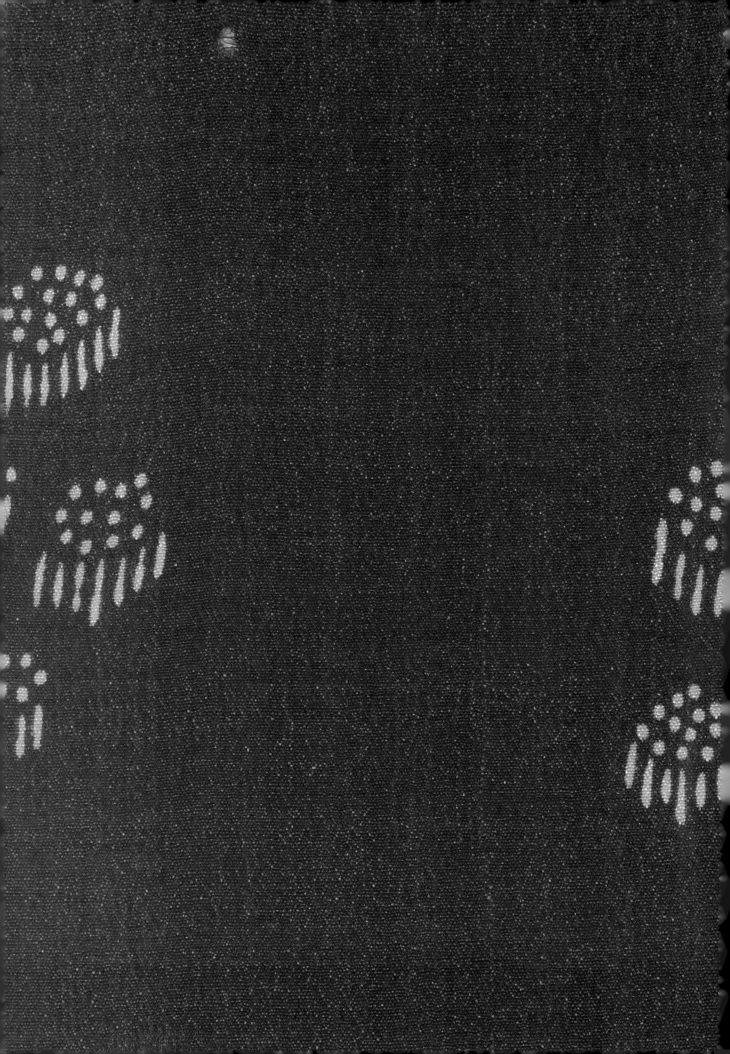

SONIA DELAUNAY
DESIGNS FOR
METZ & CO

MATTEO DE LEEUW-DE MONTI

"On Metz & Co rests the task of helping artists to realize their inspirations and bring them to the public as a finished product. Metz & Co thereby continues to build on principles which grow and evolve slowly, but which are inevitably identified with the course of life."

— Hendrik de Leeuw

FIG. 1. Hendrik de Leeuw, 1950. Private collection

FIG. 2. Joseph de Leeuw, 1935. Private collection

FIG. 3. Metz & Co, Amsterdam, the Netherlands, ca. 1960. Private collection

PREVIOUS PAGE: Design 957. France, 1929. Produced by Metz & Co, 1930. Block-printed silk. Private collection

My father, Hendrik de Leeuw (1908–1978) (FIG. 1), spoke these words at the 1952 opening of an exhibition with new fabrics by Sonia Delaunay. They articulate the basic vision of his policy and that of my grandfather, Joseph de Leeuw (1872–1944) (FIG. 2), as owners and directors of the Dutch department store Metz & Co. It was founded in the Jewish quarter in Amsterdam in the second part of the eighteenth century by merchants from the town of Metz, in Lorraine, and started out as a wholesale trader in French silks and luxury textiles. My grandfather was a self-made man from a modest Jewish background, and in 1886, when he was thirteen, he began working as an apprentice at Metz & Co. A clever businessman with a wide range of interests, including music, literature, and art, he quickly made his way up in the firm, eventually becoming associate in 1896 and director in 1910. Inspired by the aesthetics of William Morris and the Arts & Crafts movement, he began cooperating in 1902 with the English firm Liberty & Co., which was famous for its fabrics and artist-designed works. To Metz & Co he added exclusive Arts & Crafts, furniture, and fashion departments, and moved the store to its stately premises on the Leidsestraat in Amsterdam, where it remains today (FIG. 3).

In 1922, at the age of fifty and now owner of the firm, Joseph de Leeuw started to commission fabric and furniture designs from artists and architects for his own production.[1] His motives were not financial — on the contrary, other departments compensated the losses — but arose from the need to create his own style, bring art and design into daily life, and search for new forms. Alvar Aalto, Marcel Breuer, Le Corbusier, Ludwig Mies van der Rohe, Josef Hoffmann and the Wiener Werkstätte, and René Lalique are but a few of the artists whose designs were sold by Metz & Co and later became household names. After the war, Hendrik de Leeuw carried on the strategy of working with influential artists

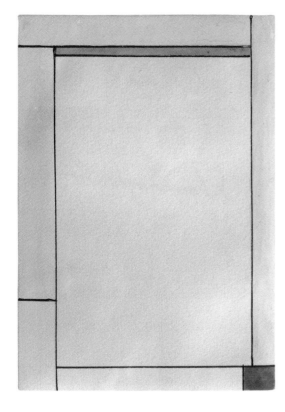

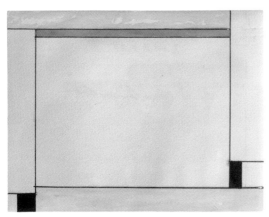

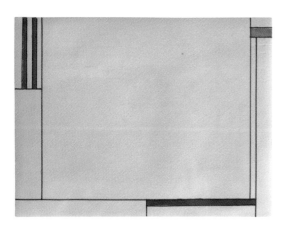

FIG. 4. Design for a Rug nos. 7, 3, 2. Designed by Georges Vantongerloo (Belgian, 1886–1965). France, 1936. Produced by Metz & Co, 1937. Gouache and ink on cardboard. Private collection

and designers, including Franco Albini, Carlo Pagani, Gio Ponti, Charles Eames, Arne Jacobsen, Marimekko, Eero Saarinen, Venini, Poul Kjaerholm, Florence Knoll, and Harry Bertoia. But the greatest stamp on the Metz style was made by three different artists: the architect and designer Gerrit Rietveld, with his ingenious solutions for matter and space; the painter Bart van der Leck, with his overwhelmingly pure color spectrum; and Sonia Delaunay, whose strong personality, powerful designs, and friendship meant much to Metz & Co and my family for years.

Rietveld and Van der Leck were both associated with De Stijl, the art magazine and movement founded in 1917 by painter and architect Theo van Doesburg (1883–1931),[2] in which a utopian ideal of geometric, non-objective painting and architecture was sought by using only straight horizontal and vertical lines, squares and rectangles, primary colors, and black and white. Among the early contributors to De Stijl were also the architect J. J. P. Oud[3] (1890–1963), Georges Vantongerloo[4] (1886–1965), Vilmos Huszar[5] (1884–1960), and of course the painter Piet Mondrian (1872–1944). Some years later, when most of the original artists had already broken with Van Doesburg, and his De Stijl rules became less rigorous, the German artist Friedrich Vordemberghe-Gildewart[6] (1899–1962) joined the group. With the exception of Mondrian and Van Doesburg, all of these artists designed for Metz & Co (FIGS. 4, 5, 6).

When De Stijl was founded, Van der Leck and Mondrian as well as Joseph de Leeuw were living in Laren, a small rural village fifteen miles outside of Amsterdam. This village was a famous refuge for painters, writers, scientists, businessmen, and all sorts of idealists. When my grandfather met Mondrian and Van der Leck at

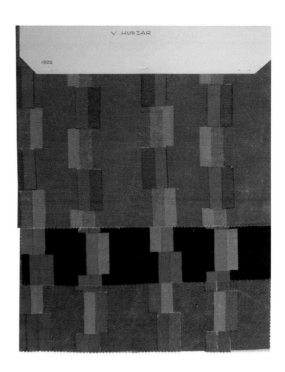

that time, they both were, similar to the Delaunays, pioneers of abstract painting, strong-willed artists, uncompromising in defending their own artistic values and truth. Van der Leck became a friend of the family. In 1918, Rietveld created what is often considered as the iconic artifact of De Stijl, the Red Blue chair, then still in its original unpainted form, and presented Van der Leck with the prototype.[7] Through Van der Leck, De Leeuw was introduced to Rietveld's work at an early and crucial stage of the latter's career.

Joseph de Leeuw first encountered the work of Sonia Delaunay at the *Exposition Internationale des Arts Décoratifs et Industriels Modernes* in Paris in 1925, where she was represented with her Boutique Simultané on the pont Alexandre III. At the time, she was designing for her enterprise, Maison Delaunay,[8] selling textile designs to a variety of firms in France and the United States, and Metz began to purchase some of her fabrics and scarves (FIG. 9). From a business collaboration, a friendship developed, and grew much more intimate after my grandmother died in 1930. At the same time, Sonia shut down her Maison Delaunay, and my grandfather commissioned her to design fabrics especially for Metz & Co. My father, who as a young man headed the fabric department, was also involved from the beginning.

From Delaunay's diaries, one gets a clear picture of the enormous care and energy she and De Leeuw *père et fils* spent working together over the years. Numerous letters, telephone calls, and countless visits were noted. In the 1930s, after working, they often went to the restaurants La Coupole or La Closerie des Lilas, where they would meet with artists such as Mondrian, Albert Gleizes, Marc Chagall, Naum Gabo, Wassily Kandinsky, Fernand Léger, Jacques Lipschitz, Antoine Pevsner, and

FIG. 5. **Metz & Co Design no. M115: fabric samples.** Designed by Vilmos Huszar (Dutch, born Hungary, 1884–1960). The Netherlands, 1922. Produced by Metz & Co. Printed linen. Private collection

FIG. 6. **Design for a Rug. Friedrich Vordemberge-Gildewart (Dutch, born Germany, 1889–1962).** The Netherlands, 1939. Gouache on ingrain wallpaper, mounted on cardboard. Private collection

FIG. 7. Design 1451. France, 1934–36. Gouache on paper, lined. Private collection

FIG. 8. Design 1176. France, 1933. Produced by Metz & Co, 1934. Gouache on paper. Private collection

FIG. 9. Design C53. France, 1924. Gouache and pencil on paper. Private collection

Vantongerloo. They enjoyed going to jazz concerts by Duke Ellington and Louis Armstrong and hearing the famous Arturo Toscanini conduct. Though very much part of the avant-garde, both the Delaunays and the De Leeuws in fact belonged to the establishment. Well connected within the art and business worlds, they were in no way "bohémiens."

From 1933 onward, Joseph de Leeuw tried to set up a new enterprise for Sonia in Paris, investing his own funds, with the idea to combine a fabric printing company with a Metz-type store, involving also designers such as Georges Bastard[9] and Jean Carlu.[10] Unfortunately, due to numerous business problems that could not be solved, the plan was abandoned in 1935. However, their attempt to set up a business together underlines the confidence they had in each other.

Throughout her life, Sonia was an artistic matchmaker. Painters like Marie Laurencin,[11] Pavel Mansouroff,[12] and Leopold Survage[13] came to design for Metz. In the 1950s, she introduced painters from the Groupe Espace, whom my father subsequently commissioned to make fabric or rug designs.[14]

**FIG. 10. Design A53 and
B53. France, 1924.**
Gouache and pencil on
paper. Private collection

**Design B53 (large version).
France, 1924.** Gouache on
paper. Private collection

VAN DER LECK AND RIETVELD

As with Delaunay, Metz & Co established loyal, long-lasting collaborations with Rietveld and Van der Leck (FIGS. 11, 12). In 1929, Van der Leck designed for Metz & Co two carpets based on his abstract paintings of 1918 (FIGS. 15 A,B).[15] At the same time, Metz produced various tubular steel chairs and tables by Rietveld. As the only non-French contributor, Metz & Co showed the works of both artists in the 1930 exhibition of the Union des Artistes Modernes[16] at the Musée des Arts Décoratifs in Paris, in which Delaunay also took part (FIGS. 17, 28).

Over a period of twenty-five years, Bart van der Leck designed a number of rugs for Metz & Co, some of which were put into production, others as one-time commissions for specific clients (FIG. 18). After leaving De Stijl within a few months of its founding, Van der Leck the painter returned to his reductive, figurative style—flat squares, rectangles, and triangles, using primary colors and black and gray on a light ground—but in his rug designs for Metz, his compositions remained abstract (FIGS. 16A,B). Unlike Sonia Delaunay, Van der Leck never made fabric designs per se, but created the colors and the color spectrum for plain furniture, interior, and dress fabrics throughout the years. In 1934, he collaborated with Rietveld on the new interior of the Metz branch in The Hague, and in 1951 on the renovation of the fabric department in Amsterdam (FIG. 27). In determining the color and applying colored areas which were spatially balanced, his goal as a painter was to create an architectonic entity, not a mere decorative solution.[17] His last design for Metz & Co was in 1952, when he created a new logo, which for many years was used on its paper gift bags and carton boxes (FIG. 13). Delaunay met Van der Leck on her first trip to Holland in 1933 and again in 1934. Interestingly, when Metz exhibited Delaunay's fabrics in 1934, in Rietveld's cupola on the roof of the building, several Dutch newspapers commented on the influence of Van der Leck on her colors (FIGS. 30, 31).[18]

As important as Van der Leck was for color, Rietveld was equally so for the interior design and architecture of the Metz & Co buildings. The idea of creating a glass-and-steel extension on top of a late nineteenth-century building in 1933 was daring and progressive. The "Koepel" (which was not really a cupola in the true sense as it had a flat roof) became an important exhibition

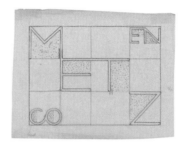

FIG. 11. Design for Metz & Co Delivery Car. Designed by Bart van der Leck (Dutch, 1876–1958). The Netherlands, 1930. Gouache and pencil on tracing paper. *Private collection*

FIG. 12. Metz & Co lettering design. Designed by Gerrit Rietveld (Dutch, 1888–1964). The Netherlands, ca. 1938. Pencil and ink on tracing paper. *Private collection*

FIG. 13. Gift bag: Metz & Co/Amsterdam/ Den Haag. Designed by Bart van der Leck (Dutch, 1876–1958). The Netherlands, 1952. Black and red ink on off-white paper, screen-printed; string. Cooper-Hewitt, National Design Museum, Smithsonian Institution, Gift of Ms. June Braun and Mr. Robert Leibowits, 1994-63-2,4,5

place for modern furniture and fabrics, floating in space with a spectacular view over Amsterdam (FIG. 19). The interior of the Metz building in The Hague followed in 1934; in 1938, Rietveld designed Metz's newly acquired *"Meubelhuis"* ("Furniture House"), originally an old canal house, a few houses away from the main building. In 1949, Hendrik de Leeuw commissioned Rietveld to totally redesign the ground floor of the main building, bringing new dimensions of space and light to the store (FIG. 14); other departments followed in 1951.

In 1932, Rietveld created one of his most famous designs, the Zig-Zag chair (FIGS. 20, 21). Metz & Co produced this revolutionary chair in many forms and in different materials for nearly forty years. Rietveld, who did not like the idea of a "finished" product, continued to explore and develop his designs. In 1938, Metz produced a rounded, laminated version. In 1940, Metz exhibited Zig-Zag chairs with armrests and round holes in the backrest as well as a Zig-Zag table (FIG. 22). There is a variant of the Red-Blue chair (FIG. 24)

in which the square slats are smoothed out and rounded off (FIG. 23, 25), as well as tubular steel versions. For Metz, he designed his *Kratmeubelen* ("crate furniture") in 1934, and in 1935 his first fully upholstered easy chair (R31). The Italian firm Cassina, which acquired Rietveld's reproduction rights in the 1970s, still uses this Rietveld/Metz design. In the course of thirty years, more than seventy-five Rietveld designs were produced by Metz & Co (FIG. 26).[19] His last design Metz executed was the 1963 Steltman chair. Metz made the original two chairs, left- and right-handed versions, upholstered in white imitation leather.[20]

FIG. 14. Metz & Co storefront with windows designed by Gerrit Rietveld, Amsterdam, the Netherlands, ca. 1949.
Private collection

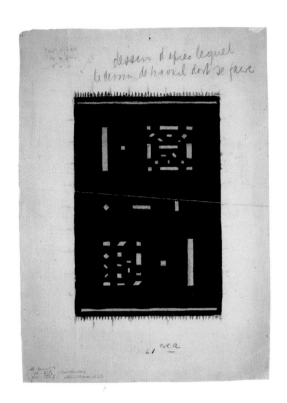

FIG. 15. A–B Designs for Rugs L1, L2. Designed by Bart van der Leck (Dutch, 1876–1958). The Netherlands, 1918. Produced by Metz & Co, 1929. Gouache and pencil on paper. Private collection

FIG. 16. A–B Designs for Rugs. Designed by Bart van der Leck (Dutch, 1876–1958). The Netherlands, 1930–39. Watercolor and pencil on paper. Private collection

FIG. 17. Metz & Co display with Van der Leck rugs and Rietveld furniture, *L'art moderne, cadre de la vie contemporaine* **exhibition of the Union des Artistes Modernes, Musée des Arts Décoratifs, Paris, 1930.** Private collection

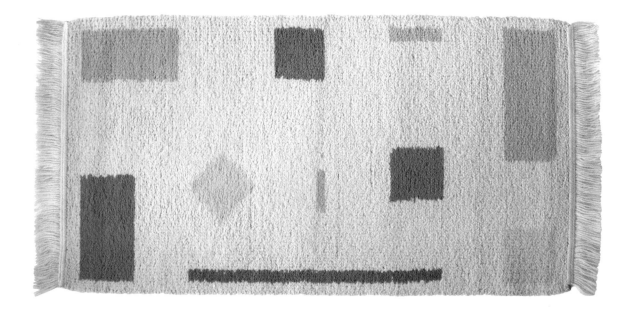

FIG. 18. Reversible rug. Designed by Bart van der Leck (Dutch, 1876–1958). Manufactured by Veneta for Metz & Co. The Netherlands, 1937, revised and reissued 1951. Private collection

FIG. 19. Opening exhibition of the Gerrit Rietveld cupola with furniture designed by Rietveld, Metz & Co, Amsterdam, the Netherlands, 1933. Private collection

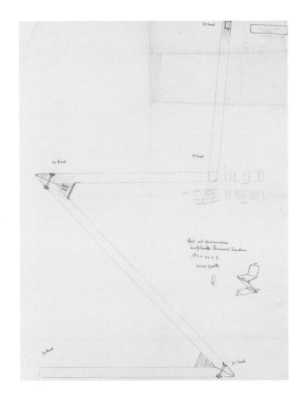

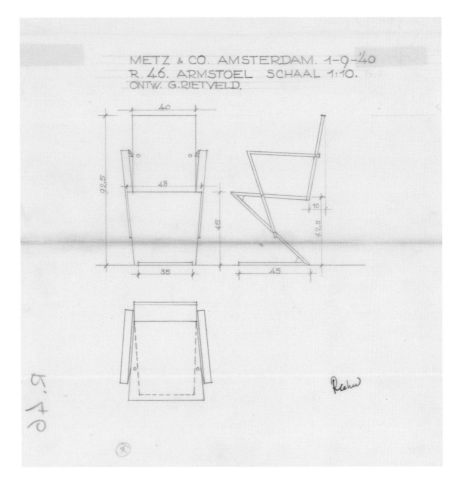

FIG. 20. 1:1 scale drawing: **Zig-Zag chair (R-18).** Designed by Gerrit Rietveld (Dutch, 1888–1964). The Netherlands, 1932–34. Pencil and ink on tracing paper. Private collection

FIG. 21. **Zig-Zag chair. Designed by Gerrit Rietveld (Dutch, 1888–1964).** The Netherlands, 1934. Oak, brass fittings. Museum of Modern Art, New York 405.1988. Image © The Museum of Modern Art/Licensed by SCALA/Art Resource, New York

FIG. 22. 1:10 scale drawing: **Zig-Zag armchair (R-46). Designed by Gerrit Rietveld (Dutch, 1888–1964).** The Netherlands, 1940. Pencil and ink on tracing paper. Private collection

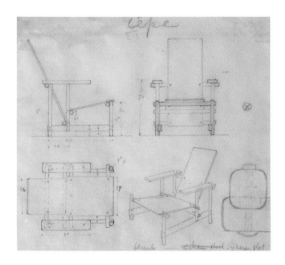

FIG. 23. 1:10 scale drawing: Red/Blue Chair with Rounded Slats. Designed by Gerrit Rietveld (Dutch, 1888–1964). The Netherlands, 1918–23. Pencil on tracing paper. Private collection

FIG. 24. Red Blue chair. Designed by Gerrit Rietveld (Dutch, 1888–1964). The Netherlands, ca. 1923. Painted wood. Museum of Modern Art, New York 487.1953. Image © The Museum of Modern Art/Licensed by SCALA/ Art Resource, New York

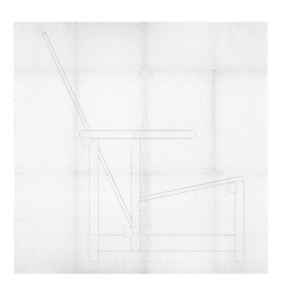

FIG. 25. 1:1 scale drawing: Red/Blue Chair with Rounded Slats. Designed by Gerrit Rietveld (Dutch, 1888–1964). The Netherlands, 1918–23. Aniline graphite pencil on paper. Private collection

FIG. 26. Design drawing: Cupboards and Table for Living Room. Designed by Gerrit Rietveld (Dutch, 1888–1964). The Netherlands, 1952. Colored pencil and ink on lined paper. Private collection

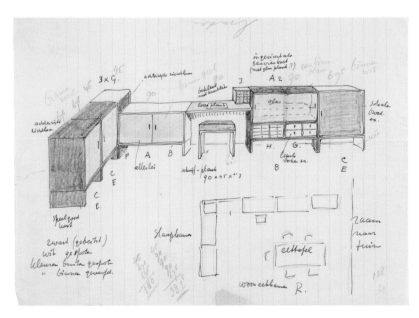

THE LEGACY OF METZ AND CO

In 1973, after nearly a half century at Metz, my father decided to retire and sold the firm.[21] At home we kept our private Metz archive, and I remember distinctly how my father and I browsed through a fabric book with designs by Vilmos Huszar, Marie Laurencin, and Sonia Delaunay — marvelous designs, beautiful fabrics (FIG. 29). "But that doesn't interest anyone anymore these days," my father said. Metz had become history for us.

So for some years to come, our family archives lay patiently in the cellar next to the boiler and the washing machine. A few years after my father's death in 1978, my mother had a visit from Petra Timmer, a young art historian, who wanted to write her dissertation about Metz & Co in the 1930s. She ended up dedicating her doctorate to the work of my father and grandfather. Apart from our private archive, she studied the very comprehensive Metz archives, which at that time were stored in the bell tower of the main building in Amsterdam. In 1986, a total conversion of the building took place and everything had to be cleared out. The directors at that time, contrary to the current management, were in no way interested in the dusty archives. Thanks to Petra Timmer's efforts, however, the archives were preserved. The Metz archives now reside at the Municipal Archives of Amsterdam and the Amsterdam Historic Museum.[22] Her enthusiasm was catching, inspiring me to delve again into the material and rediscover the many artists that found a forum for their creativity at Metz & Co, especially Sonia Delaunay, whom I personally had known so well. Together with the Metz fabric books, I studied Delaunay's *livres noirs*, the design books in which she had recorded her designs of the 1920s and 1930s and had access to her *Journaux* at the Bibliothèque Nationale in Paris. Through her observations I learned a lot about my family, commercially and privately. Her diary entries were sometimes touching, occasionally very critical, and extremely revealing. I was more than amused when I finally had written proof that my grandfather had indeed wanted to marry her.[23] I found answers to many questions I had never been able to ask, either to Sonia or my father. More important, it became very clear that, in the 1940s and 1950s, Delaunay devoted herself more to fabric designs than is usually

acknowledged. Her designs for Metz & Co as well as for firms such as Heim, Flachard, and Perrier[24] during that period obviously prove this.

What formerly was considered working material, and not works of art in themselves, gained a totally new significance. Rumpled textile designs and samples have been conserved and catalogued and the correspondence compiled. In the end, I developed an unexpected view of Sonia Delaunay's indefatigable creative talent (FIGS. 32–48). This resulted in the *Sonia Delaunay — Metz est venu* exhibition at the Stedelijk Museum in Amsterdam, the first of many exhibitions devoted to her work and commitment to Metz & Co.[25]

Sonia was never a designer in the usual sense. Her designs were not subject to the whims of fashion. They are timeless. She remained a painter, a universal artist who applied her art onto fabrics. "I always changed everything around me," Sonia said. "I made my first white walls so our paintings would look better. I designed my furniture; I have done everything. I have lived my art."

FIG. 27. Metz & Co Fabric Department. Designed by Gerrit Rietveld and Bart van der Leck. Amsterdam, the Netherlands, 1951. Private collection

FIG. 28. Sonia Delaunay display, *L'art moderne, cadre de la vie contemporaine* **exhibition of the Union des Artistes Modernes, Musée des Arts Décoratifs, Paris, 1930.** Private collection

FIG. 29. Metz & Co fabric book, machine print (Designs 501–41), with Design 965. France, 1929–34. Colorprint, gouache, ink, and pencil on paper. Private collection

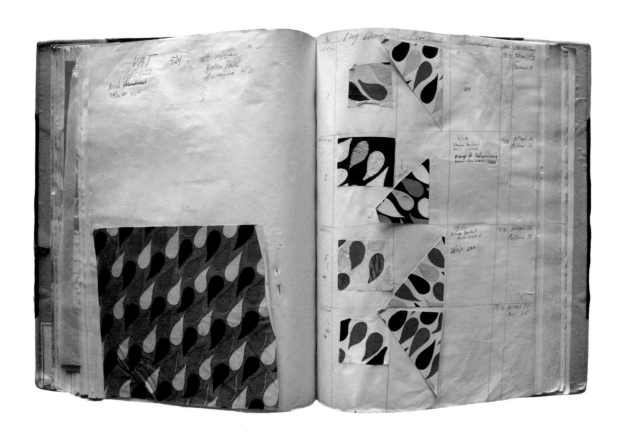

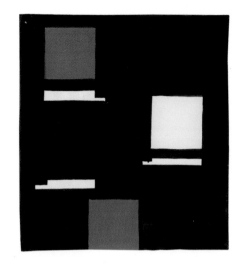

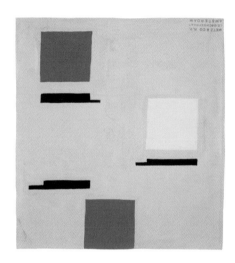

FIG. 30. Exhibition of Sonia Delaunay fabrics in the Rietveld cupola, Metz & Co, Amsterdam, the Netherlands, 1934. Private collection

FIG. 31. A–D Design 1177. France, 1933. Produced by Metz & Co, 1934. Gouache on paper. Private collection

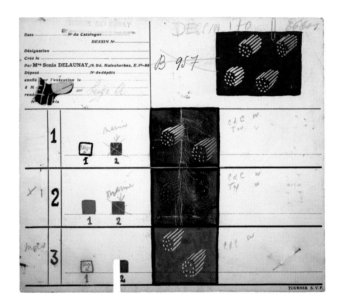

FIG. 32. Design 957: working drawing, textile design, design card, fabric samples. France, 1929. Produced by Metz & Co, 1930. Gouache on tracing paper; gouache, ink, and pencil on paper; gouache, ink, and pencil on paper, with fabric swatch; block-printed silk. Private collection

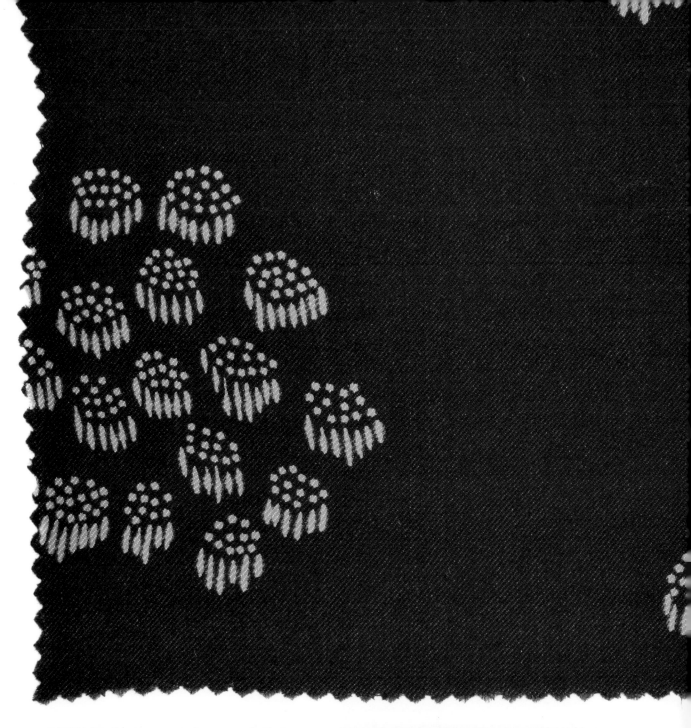

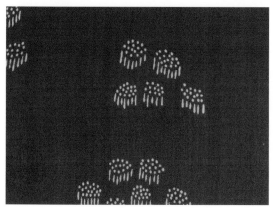
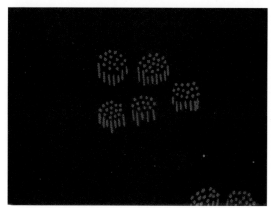

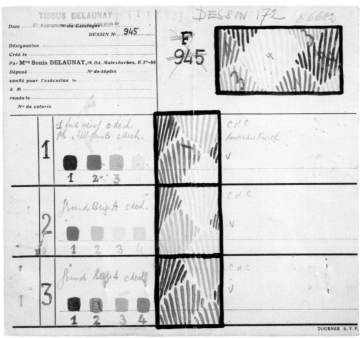

FIG. 33. Design 945: textile design, design card, fabric samples. France, 1929. Produced by Metz & Co, 1930. Gouache, ink, and pencil on paper; gouache, ink, and pencil on paper; printed silk. Private collection

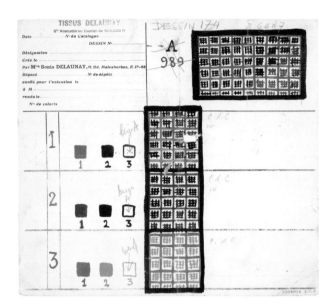

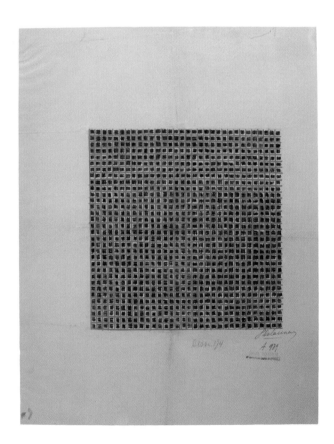

FIG. 34. Design 989A: design card, textile design, fabric samples. France, 1930. Gouache, ink, and pencil on paper; printed silk swatches on cardboard header. Private collection

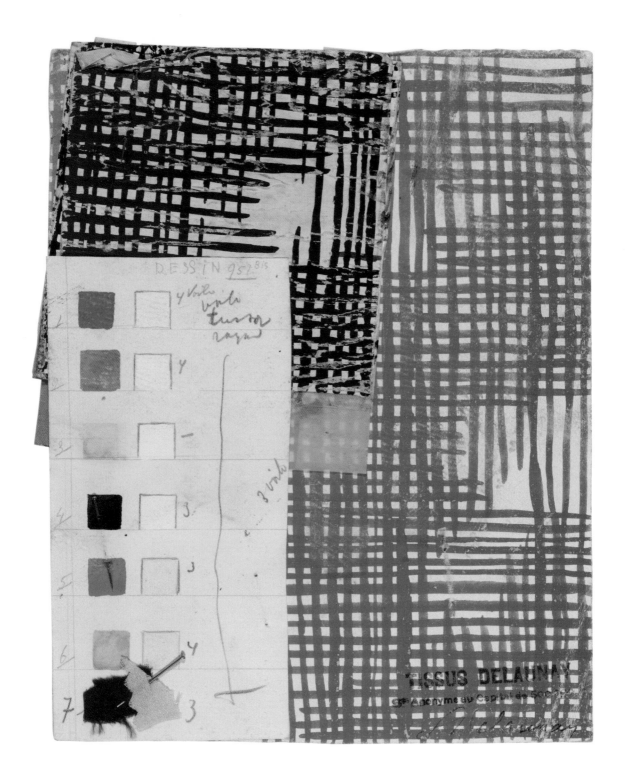

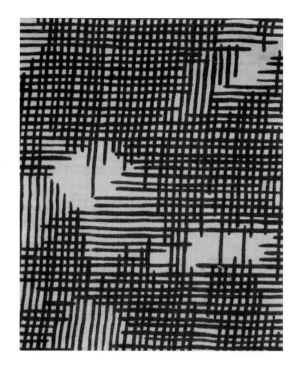
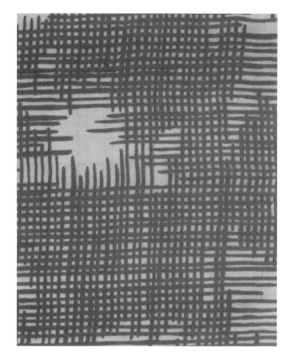
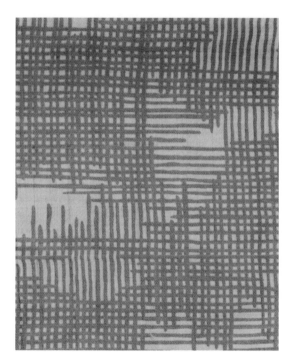
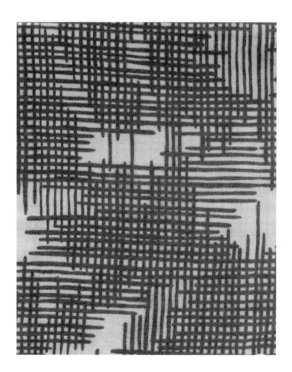

FIG. 35. Design 951bis: textile design, fabric samples. France, 1929. Produced by Metz & Co, 1930. Gouache, ink, and pencil on paper; printed silk. Private collection

FIG. 36. Design 965: textile designs, fabric samples. France, 1930. Produced by Metz & Co, Gouache on tracing paper, lined; printed cotton. Private collection

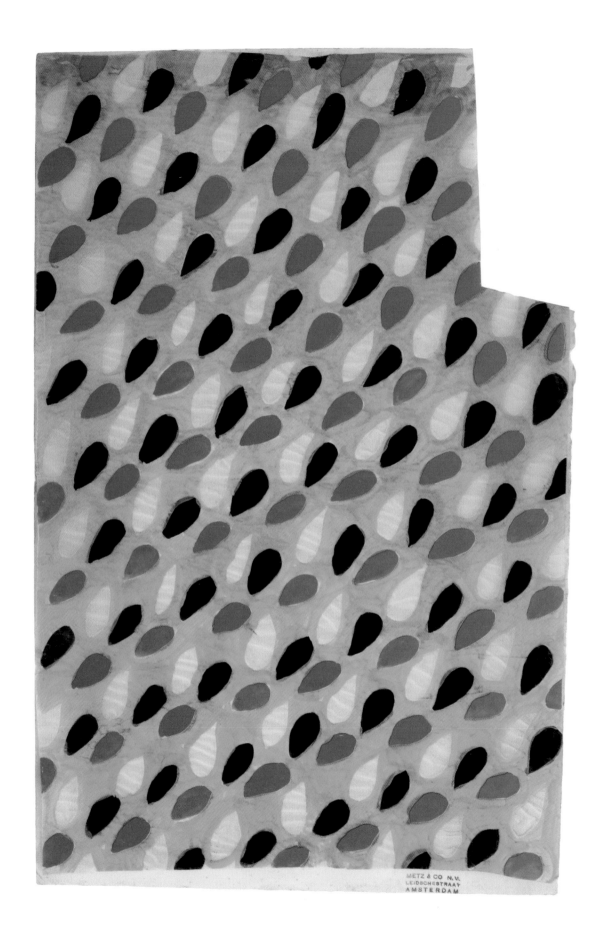

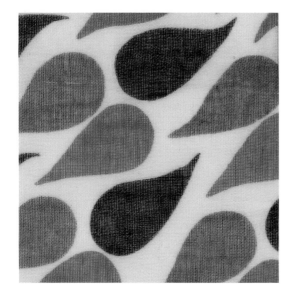

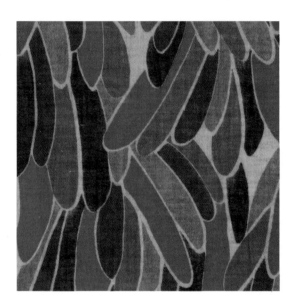
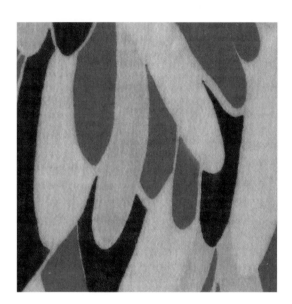

FIG. 37. Design 1044: textile designs, fabric samples. France, 1930. Produced by Metz & Co, 1931. Gouache and pencil on tracing paper; printed cotton georgette. Private collection

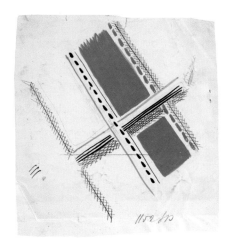

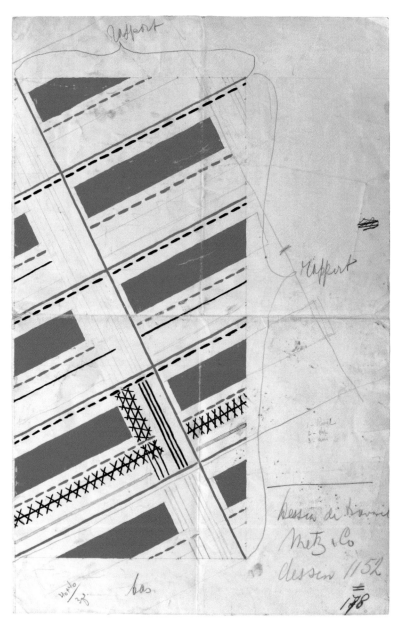

FIG. 38. **Design 1152:
working drawing, textile
design, fabric samples.**
France, 1932. Produced by
Metz & Co, 1933. Gouache
and pencil on paper;
printed silk. Private collection

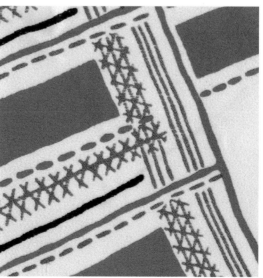

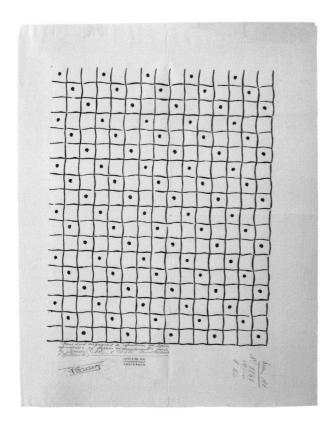

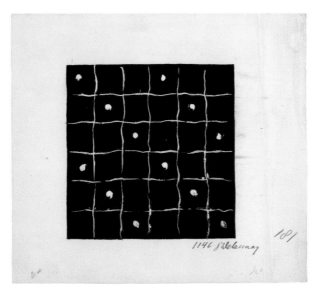

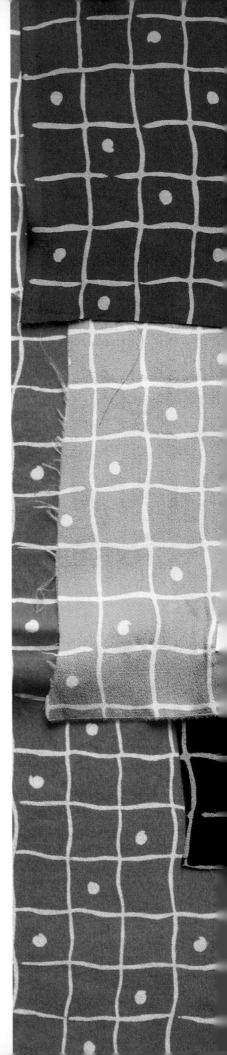

FIG. 39. Design 1146: master print, textile design, fabric samples. France, 1932. Produced by Metz & Co, 1933. Printed by Petitdidier. Colorprint; gouache, ink, and pencil on paper; printed silk. Private collection

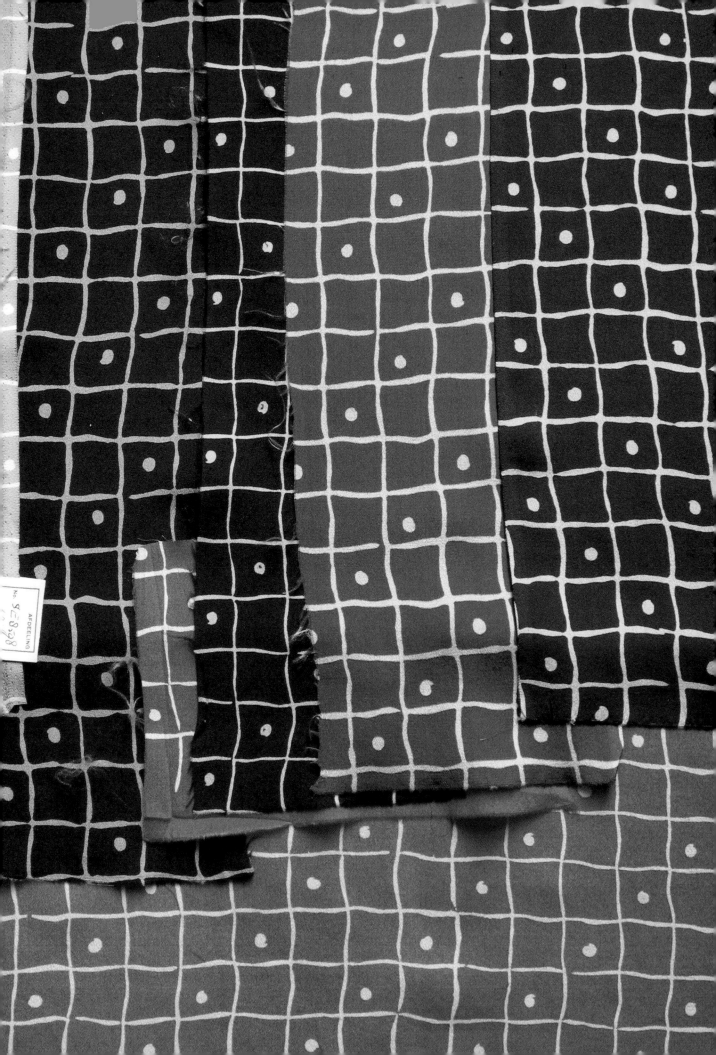

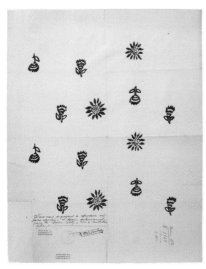

FIG. 40. Design 1147:
textile design, master print,
sketch, fabric samples.
France, 1932. Produced by
Metz & Co, 1933. Printed
by Petitdidier. Gouache and
pencil on paper; colorprint,
pencil, and ink on paper;
gouache and ink on paper;
printed silk. Private collection

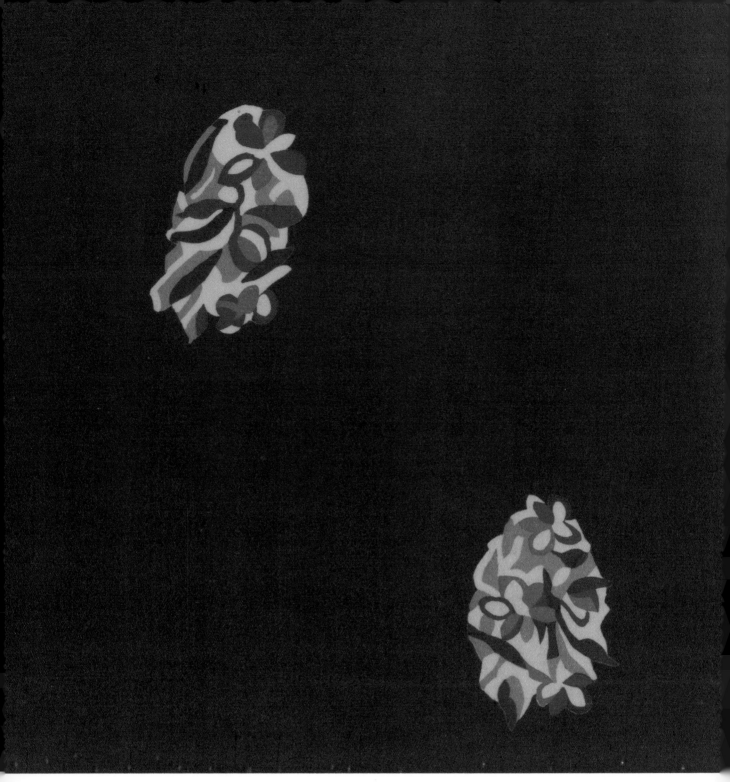

FIG. 41. **Design 1257: fabric sample, working drawings, textile design.** France, 1933. Produced by Metz & Co. Printed silk; gouache, ink, and pencil on paper; gouache on paper; gouache and pencil on paper. Private collection

FIG. 42. Design 1219: textile designs, fabric sample. France, 1933. Produced by Metz & Co. Gouache on tracing paper; printed silk mousseline. Private collection

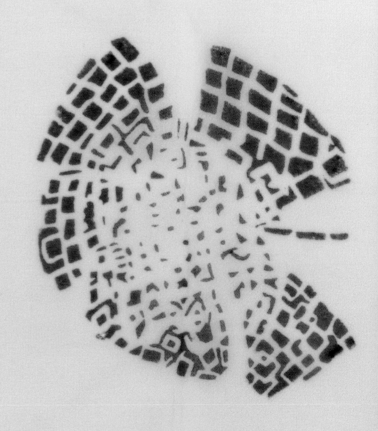

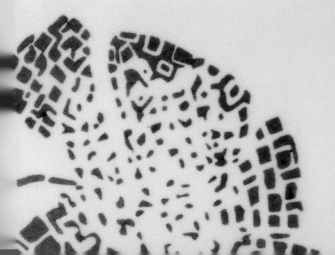

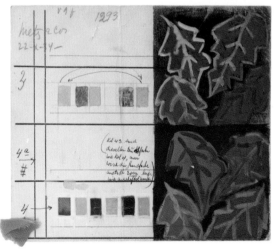

**FIG. 43. Design 1293:
sketches, design card,
textile design, fabric
samples. France, 1934.**
Produced by Metz & Co.
Gouache and pencil on
paper; gouache, ink and
pencil on paper, lined;
printed cotton georgette.
Private collection

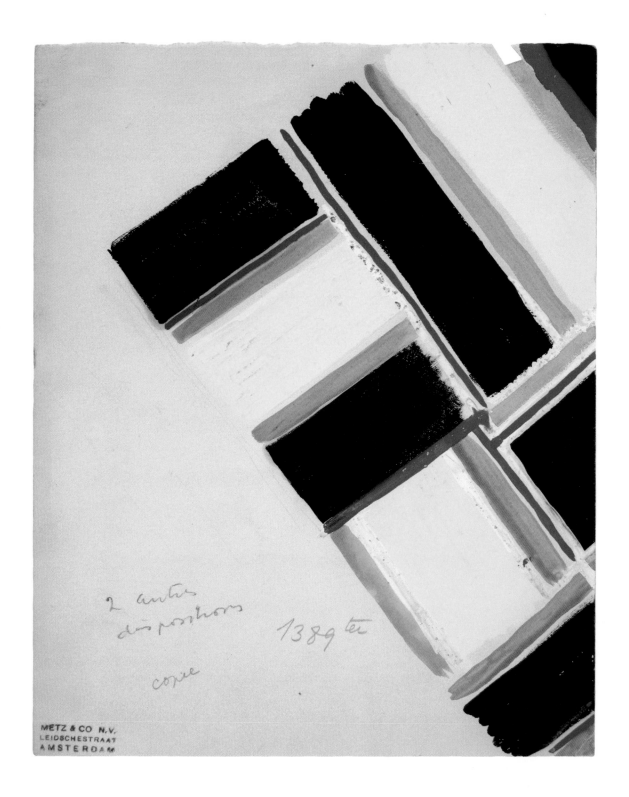

FIG. 44. Variation on Design 1355. France, 1934. Gouache on paper.
Private collection

FIG. 45. Design 1389. France, 1934. Produced by Metz & Co, 1936. Gouache, pencil, and ink on paper.
Private collection

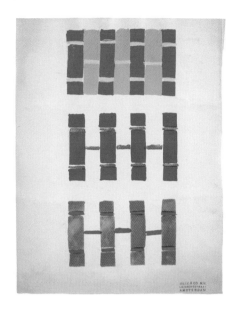
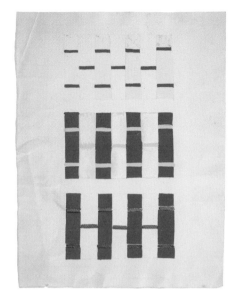
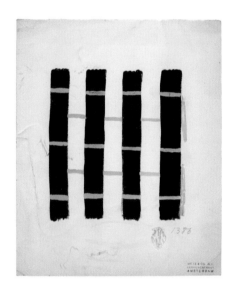

FIG. 46. Design 1386: textile designs, fabric samples. France, 1934. Produced by Metz & Co, 1936. Gouache on paper; printed silk crêpe de chine. Private collection

**FIG. 47. Design 1391: textile
design, fabric sample.**
France, 1934. Produced by
Metz & Co, 1936. Gouache
on paper; printed silk.
Private collection

SE 6000

SE 6001

FIG. 48. Design 198: fabric samples. France, 1927. Produced by Metz & Co, 1936. Printed silk crêpe de chine. Private collection

SE 6002

NOTES

PAGE 107

1   By 1918, De Leeuw already employed Dutch furniture designer Paul Bromberg.

PAGE 108

2   Van Doesburg and the Delaunays knew each other well. Van Doesburg's wife, Nelly, became a friend of Sonia's. They both fought hard to garner recognition for their husbands' careers.

3   J. J. P. Oud was a Dutch architect and Municipal Housing Architect of Rotterdam (1918–33). At the time, he was considered one of Europe's four most important architects, along with Walter Gropius, Ludwig Mies van der Rohe, and Le Corbusier. In the 1930s, he made several furniture designs for Metz & Co.

4   Georges Vantongerloo, Belgian-born painter and sculptor. After a few years in Holland, he moved to Paris, where he became friends with the Delaunays. In 1931, he set up the movement Abstraction-Création, which the Delaunays joined. Joseph de Leeuw knew him personally for years. In 1937, he designed a series of rugs for Metz & Co based on his mathematical paintings. Later in life he experimented with new forms and material, including Plexiglas.

5   Vilmos Huszar, Hungarian painter and designer who moved to Holland. After De Stijl, he also joined the Dada movement. A very versatile artist, he made one of the first fabrics Joseph de Leeuw commissioned in 1922, and designed furniture for Metz & Co in the 1930s.

6   Friedrich Vordemberghe-Gildewart (1899–1962), German abstract painter, architect, and designer. After joining De Stijl, he was a member of Cercle et Carré and Abstraction-Création with Vantongerloo and the Delaunays. In Germany, his work was considered *Entartete Kunst* (degenerate art), which is why he immigrated to Holland, where he lived until 1954. For Metz & Co he designed a series of rugs in 1939. In the 1950s he headed the Hochschule für Gestaltung Ulm.

PAGE 109

7   This chair remained with the Van der Leck family until 1986, when it was auctioned at Christie's. Rietveld made the color version in 1923.

8   Sonia Delaunay had registered her fabric and fashion enterprise under the name of "Sonia" in March 1925. She then trademarked the word "Simultané" (in the United States on April 18, 1925) and on December 28, 1926, the name "Sonia Delaunay." Her workshop was referred to as the "Atelier Simultané" and her enterprise as "Maison Delaunay." On January 1, 1929, she registered under "Tissus Delaunay."

PAGE 110

9   Georges Bastard (1881–1939) was a French designer who worked especially in wood- and metalwork, ivory, tortoise, and fans. His objects were sold at Metz & Co.

10 Jean Carlu (1900–1997) was a French graphic designer and commercial artist. Like his colleague A.-M. Cassandre, he designed catalog covers for Metz & Co.

11 Marie Laurencin (1883–1956) was a French painter, especially of portraits, and designer (f.i. for Diaghilev). She had an intense love affair with the poet Guillaume Apollinaire, a great friend of the Delaunays. She made three fabric designs for Metz & Co.

12 Pavel Mansouroff (1896–1983) was a Russian avant-garde painter and designer, associated with Malevich at the INKHUK and GINKHUK. Delaunay helped him for years by providing him with work and a studio. He designed many fabrics and rugs for Metz & Co.

13 Leopold Survage (1879–1968) was a Russian painter and designer who was introduced to the Delaunays by Apollinaire. He called his early work *Rythme Coloré*, a term generally associated with the Delaunays. For the 1937 Expo, he collaborated with Delaunay on the Palais de Chemin de Fer (Railroad Palace). He made fabric designs for Chanel and rug designs for Metz & Co.

14 Edgar Pillet, Paule Vézelay, Silvano Bozzolini, Alcopley, and, in the 1960s, Ladislas Kijno. Some of their Metz fabrics are now in the Amsterdam Historical Museum.

PAGE 114

15 The only surviving original carpet to my knowledge of Van der Leck's first Metz designs is in the collection of The Museum of Modern Art in New York. Since the 1980s, I have reedited these and later rug designs, some of which are now in the collection of the Stedelijk Museum, the Kröller-Müller Museum, and the Centraal Museum in the Netherlands.

16 See also *Les années UAM 1929–1958*, Les Arts Décoratifs (Paris, 1988): 117–18.

17 See *Observations by the painter B. van der Leck* (1953) and letter from Van der Leck to H. de Leeuw, March 1953.

18 *Nieuwe Rotterdamsche Courant*, April 5, 1935.

PAGE 115

19 Metz numbered Rietveld's designs with the initial R. R1 was Rietveld's first *Beugelstoel*. The first Zig-Zag chair was R18. The highest number I know of is a postwar table, R75; however, Rietveld's Metz documentation is not complete. The largest collection of Rietveld drawings is in the Rietveld-Schröder Archives in Utrecht. The Centraal Museum in Utrecht and the Stedelijk Museum in Amsterdam have the largest collection of Rietveld furniture. The Victoria & Albert Museum in London has drawings of Rietveld's crate furniture.

20 The two original Steltman chairs are in the collection of the Kröller-Müller Museum in Otterlo.

PAGE 120

21 In 1973 Metz & Co was sold to Liberty's. It has passed hands several times since.

22 Metz & Co has now donated the fabric collection to the Amsterdam Historic Museum. The Metz & Co archive at the Municipal Archives of Amsterdam, comprised of Metz's historical administration, correspondence, designs, publicity, and photographs, is now considered one of the finest examples of its kind.

23 Journal Sonia Delaunay, 22 September 1948.

24 Jacques Heim (1899–1967) managed his parents' fur fashion house in the twenties. In 1925, he set up the Boutique Simultané with Sonia Delaunay. In 1930, he opened his own couture house, Heim, and edited the *Revue Heim*. He dressed Mme Charles de Gaulle and Mrs. Dwight D. Eisenhower. Maison Heim closed in 1969.

Flachard, a famous fabric manufacturer based in Lyon, had a branch on the Rue de la Paix in Paris. It closed in the 1970s. Robert Perrier (1898–1987) provided many of the famous couturiers with his fabrics. A friend of the Delaunays, he produced a number of Sonia's fabrics in the 1940s and also acquired from her a collection of her fabric designs. Perrier closed in 1967.

25 Below is a list of exhibitions to date featuring Sonia Delaunay's designs for Metz & Co:

Sonia Delaunay–Metz est venu, Stedelijk Museum, Amsterdam, the Netherlands, 1992

Sonia Delaunay en Hollande, Institut Néerlandais, Paris, 1993; Musée de la Tapisserie, Tournai, Belgium, 1994–95

Sonia Delaunay–dissenys tèxtils holandesos, Fundació La Caixa, Barcelona-Granollers, Spain, 1995

Sonia Delaunay–Textildesign 1930–1960, Städtische Kunstsammlungen, Chemnitz, Germany, 1996

Metz & Co–De Creatieve Jaren, Stedelijk Museum, Amsterdam, 1995–96

Metz & Co–los años creativos, IVAM, Valencia, Spain, 1996

Sonia Delaunay–Tecidos Simultaneos, Museu Nacional de Soares dos Reis, Oporto 2001–2

Sonia Delaunay's Welt der Kunst, Kunsthalle Bielefeld, Bielefeld, Germany, 2008–9

DATING SONIA DELAUNAY'S FABRIC DESIGNS

MATTEO DE LEEUW-DE MONTI

When I initially started to catalog and date Sonia Delaunay's designs for Metz & Co, I was confronted with two different problems. First, as Delaunay was by no means the only artist designing fabrics for Metz & Co, I had to make sure that her work was identified and attributed correctly. Second, in nearly every book written on Delaunay and in every exhibition about her, it has been noted that she stopped designing in 1930 with the closing of her Maison Delaunay and returned solely to painting.[1] Paradoxically, and with only a few rare exceptions, in all the publications on Sonia Delaunay there were never any images of paintings between 1930 and 1935, whereas she designed in abundance for Metz & Co during this period. Even in *Nous irons jusqu'au soleil* (*We Shall Go Up to the Sun*), the autobiography Delaunay wrote in collaboration with Jacques Damase, who managed her in the late 1960s and 1970s, there is a noticeable gap in her career during the 1930s. This easily led to the misinterpretation that what Delaunay called her "years of liberation" began in 1930 as opposed to 1936, when she began concentrating on painting again. This could have also led to the incorrect conclusion that she stopped designing fabrics after 1930.

My first source for designs created before 1940 was Metz's own fabric books, from which I established the designer, design numbers, date of execution, printer, and the *métrage* (yardage) — some of Sonia's fabrics were so exclusive that only thirty meters were printed (FIG. 2A). Metz was sometimes provided with numerous versions of a design: a main design in gouache, watercolor, or India ink that was signed, numbered, and sometimes dated (FIG. 2C); *a dessin de travail*, or working drawing; and various other works in different colors on transparent or heavy paper, which were unsigned and undated (FIG. 2E). I compared these to one of my main sources for dating and attributing the designs — Delaunay's own design books, bound in black linen, the *Livres noirs*[2] (FIG. 1). She began

PREVIOUS PAGE:
Design 253: collage.
France, 1928–30. Produced by Metz & Co, 1931. Collage of gouache on tracing paper, lined. Private Collection

FIG. 1. Livre noir I, page 1, Dessin no. 6. Gouache and ink on paper. Private collection

FIG. 2A. Metz & Co fabric book with Design 1317. France, 1934. Gouache and ink on paper with silk swatches. Private collection

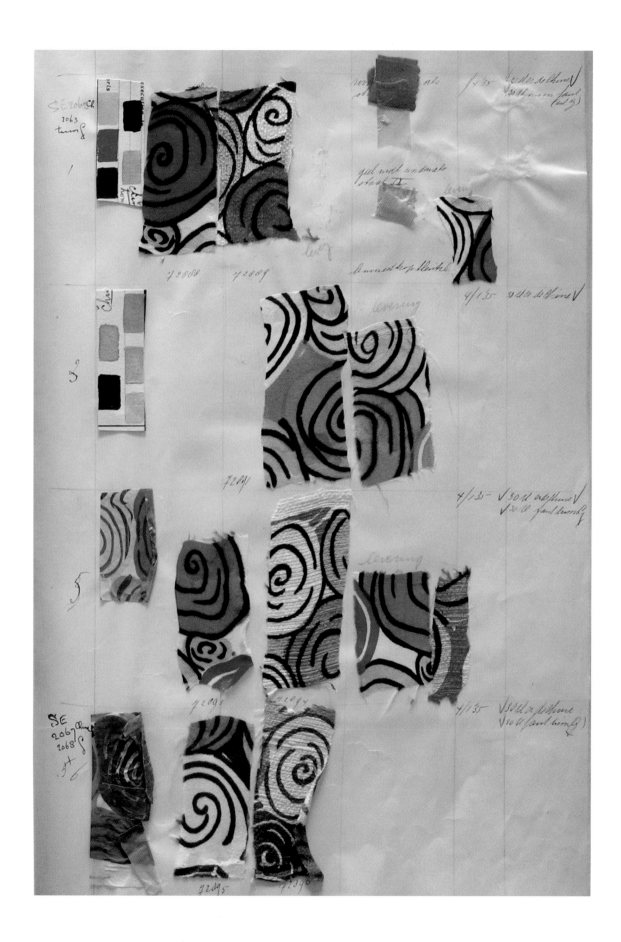

FIGS. 2B–F. Design 1317: design card, textile design, working drawing, master print, fabric sample. France, 1934. Produced by Metz & Co. Gouache, ink, and pencil on paper; gouache, ink, and pencil on paper; colorprint, pencil, and ink on paper; gouache and ink on tracing paper; printed silk crêpe de chine. Private collection

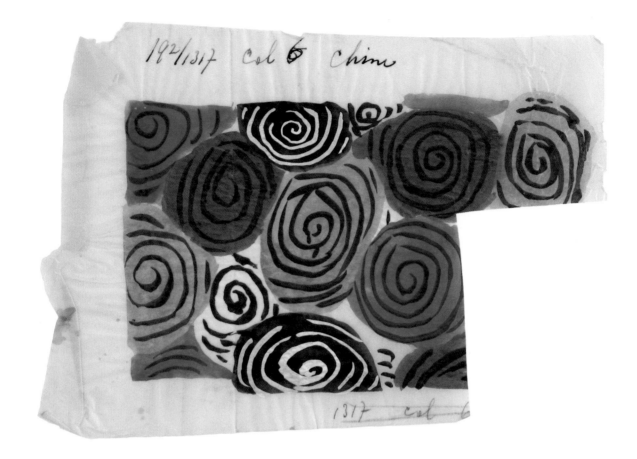

FIG. 3. Fabric sample: Design 903. France, 1929. Produced by Metz & Co, 1936. Printed silk crêpe de chine. Private collection

FIG. 4. From deposit 8338 of April 15, 1925, 20 designs for embroidery on textiles. Archives de Paris D12U10 178

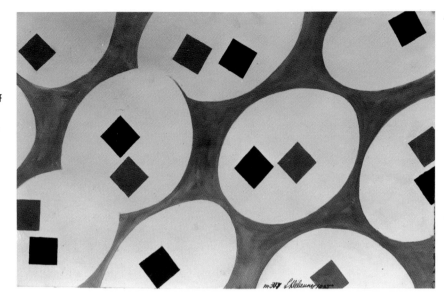

recording in these "black books" in August 1924; numbers I–IX cover the period 1924–34. Her account books and diaries, where she recorded which designs she was working on, formed the other main sources for dating. Also, her design card, the *pancarte*, often noted the design number and date, and included a small gouache and various *coloris* (color schemes) (FIG. 2B). Delaunay's name and boulevard Malesherbes address were printed on the card, and she continued to use these pancartes into the 1940s, long after she moved to the rue St. Simon in 1935. The master prints made by the printer Petitdidier confirm some of the dating for 1933–34 (FIG. 2D). For the postwar period, Delaunay's diary entries, combined with correspondence between her and my father, helped identify her later designs. Metz & Co apparently kept no fabric books at the time.

Over the years, Metz & Co bought approximately 200 designs from Delaunay, not all of which were produced. In cataloging the designs, I have often included two dates: the year of the original design, and the year in which Metz & Co bought or produced the design. When known, Delaunay's design number

is included next to Metz's own design number. In describing her designs for Metz & Co in her diaries, Delaunay makes a distinction between *dessins nouveaux* (new designs) and *dessins anciens* (old designs), which were originally made between 1924 and 1929 but reworked at a later date (FIG. 3).[3]

In *Livre noir* I, which covered the period from 1924 to 1925 and included designs numbered 1–100, Delaunay meticulously noted the design number, the date on which it was created, the date on which it was sent to the printer, the name of the engraver,[4] the company it was commissioned by or sold to,[5] and prices. During the first year in which she patented her designs, the patent registration number was also recorded. She added a black-and-white photograph of the patented designs (FIG. 4). Initially, she also kept a double numbering system reflecting a series she had created prior to recording them in her first *Livre noir*. For example, her first entry of no. 1 (lowercase) actually is Dessin No. 6 (uppercase); no. 2 is Dessin no. 7; and no. 22 (lowercase) is Dessin No. 34 (uppercase), with the designs or photographs always bearing the actual design number in uppercase letters.

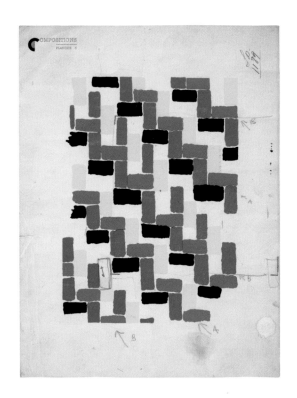

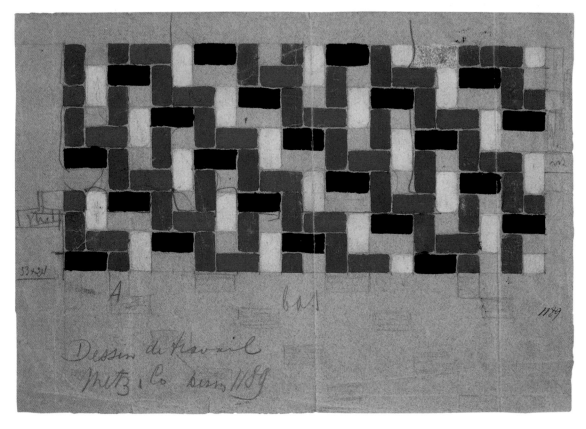

FIGS. 5A–H. Design 1189: book plate, master print, working drawing, tie, fabric samples. France, 1929. Produced by Metz & Co, 1933. Printed by Petitdidier. Pochoir on paper; colorprint, pencil, and ink on paper; gouache, ink, and pencil on paper; printed silk.
Private collection

This numeric labyrinth was simplified in *Livre noir* II (nos. 4–18 and 91–208), which included Delaunay's designs up to 1927. *Livres noirs* III and IV (nos. 209–352 and nos. 353–492 respectively) recorded designs to 1928. In her *Livre noir* V (nos. 493–622), Delaunay recorded costume sketches from various periods. For instance, design no. 503 is a sketch of a Simultaneous dress dated 1924; no. 549 is a long scarf design for Cléopâtre from 1918;[6] and no.599 is a fabric sketch from 1928. *Livre noir* VI (nos. 623–772) similarly included sketches and details of coats or dresses.

Livre noir VII (nos. 773–913) featured fabric designs from 1929; *Livre noir* VIII (nos. 913–1065), 1929–30; and *Livre noir* IX (nos. 1100–1409), fabric and dress designs from 1930–34. Occasionally, designs in the ninth *Livre noir* were based on earlier works from her *Compositions, Couleurs, Idées*[7] album and were renumbered (FIG. 5 A–H). In this book, only design numbers, clients, and invoice numbers are listed;[8] for Metz designs, she often added fabric swatches once the fabric was manufactured.

Delaunay also kept an invoice book, in which she recorded the invoice number, buyer, date, design number (with page and *Livre noir* number), and price. From this invoice book, I discovered the existence of *Livre noir* X, apparently now lost, which included designs numbered from 1410. Many of these designs (1424–1494) were purchased by Metz in 1936 and 1937, and were Delaunay's last known prewar designs. In her diaries, Sonia listed all designs sold to Metz from 1933 until 1937.[9]

It was not until 1936 that Delaunay temporarily ceased designing fabrics to concentrate on painting, after a break of nearly twenty years. She started to prepare her husband Robert's and her participation for the Paris World's Fair of 1937[10] in association with Felix

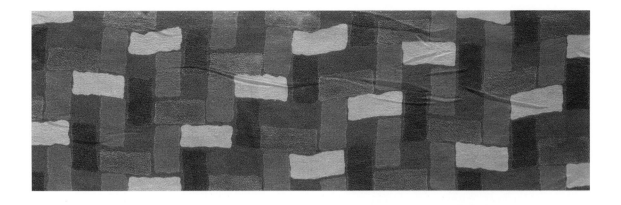

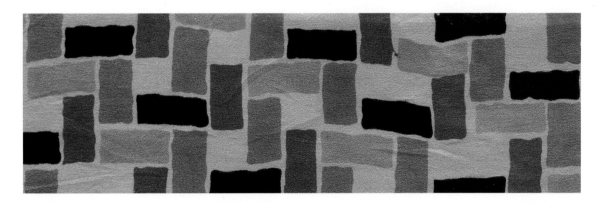

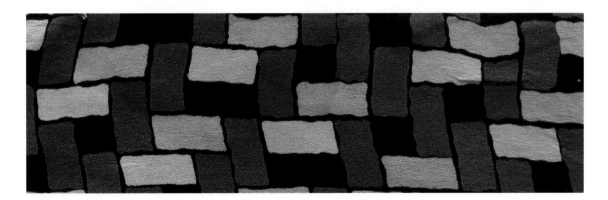

FIG. 6. **Design 485: textile design.** France, 1947. Produced by Metz & Co, 1948. Gouache and ink on tracing paper. Private collection

Aublet.[11] Also, 1938 and 1939 were years of extreme creativity after she finally returned to abstract painting (FIG. 15), but the outbreak of the war and Robert's death in 1941 abruptly halted everything.[12] Interestingly, on June 15, 1942, Delaunay noted, "Took the Metz fabrics from basket nr. 2 of the storage room."[13] When fleeing Paris in May 1940, the Delaunays had loaded their car with Robert's rolled-up paintings[14]; Sonia had also packed her Metz fabrics. Delaunay did not design for Metz during the war. Joseph de Leeuw was forced to relinquish the business he had created; he was deported, and died in a concentration camp. Hendrik de Leeuw managed to escape to the United States. He regained control of Metz after the war.

In April 1942, Delaunay made fabric designs, which she numbered 100–17, for Maison Gonnet in Lyon.[15] Two weeks later, she noted in her diary, "Sold to Perrier designs for fabrics: 100–31 (31 at 200fr=6200fr) 28 printings, 3 weaves."[16] Delaunay had started a new numbering system, beginning with no.100, which should not be confused with her numbers from her first four *Livres noirs*. In 1948, Metz bought nos. 473bis, 482, 485 and 501, which she was working on that year (FIGS. 6, 7).

Back in Paris, Delaunay started to design again in October 1945. She also began to use a new numbering system of year and design number, which makes her postwar designs easier to distinguish from her designs of the 1920s. In her diary, Delaunay wrote on October 7, 1945: "Added to the inventory design nos. 4501, 4502, 4503, 4504, 4505, 4506," which she sold to Heim.[17] Delaunay was not as prolific in the postwar years as in the 1920s and 1930s. Not only was she assiduously establishing recognition for Robert Delaunay and painting again herself, but in the aftermath of the war, silk printing and weaving facilities were limited and export was restricted.

Delaunay's first post-war designs for Metz were in 1946. She wrote on June 9, 1946: "Made 13 Fabric designs 4601–4613 (...) I started to work. Made fabric designs for Metz whilst listening to the sports news on the radio. This is my favorite program. It's lively and not stupid. Made 13 designs which came out very easily."[18]

In 1949, Delaunay started on a series of rayures (stripes), no. 4901, which were used by Heim as well as by Metz & Co (FIG. 8); Metz also produced and sold no. 4902, a large rose design, until the 1960s

FIG. 7. Design 501. France, 1948. Gouache and pencil on paper. Private collection

FIG. 8. Design 4901.
France, 1949. Gouache
and pencil on paper.
Private collection

FIG. 9. Scarf. Produced by
Liberty's of London. France,
ca. 1967. Printed silk voile.
Private collection

FIGS. 10A–D. Design 4902 Rosarium I: studies, textile design, fabrics. France, 1949–50. Produced by Metz & Co, 1950. Gouache and pencil on paper; printed linen. Private collection

FIG. 11. Design 4903 Rosarium II (right). France, 1949. Produced by Metz & Co, 1950. Gouache on paper. Private collection

FIG. 12. Scarf. Produced by Liberty's of London. France, ca. 1967. Printed silk voile. Private collection

FIG. 13. Scarf, Design 593 #3. Produced by Liberty's of London. France, 1969. Printed silk. Private collection

(FIGS. 10 A-D, 11). In addition, Metz worked with the Lyon company Flachard on nos. 4907, 4911, and 4914; other manufacturers Metz used regularly were Bucol and Leroux. Delaunay worked on Dessin no. 4939, a *carré* for Heim, and ended the year with Dessin no. 4947. In January 1950, she started on Dessins 5001–5020 for Metz,[19] and she recorded these designs in notebooks.[20] On June 12, 1951, she wrote: "I've finished designs numbered 5110 to 5118. 5110 has three variations ... Sent letter to H. de Leeuw with fifteen designs of which six are variations." This type of numbering remained continuous until the early 1950s.

Delaunay made various inventories of her work, and wrote the new number on the design. To add extra confusion to her numbering system, an inventory was made where the numbering started with an F (possibly by Boris Fraenkel, the assistant who catalogued for her in the 1950s). For example, design 501 (*Tulipes*) of 1948 is also F5206; and design 4902 (*Roses*) of 1949 is F5207.[21] The number following the F does not refer to the date.

By the mid-1950s, Delaunay had started to become well established as a painter, and announced to Hendrik de Leeuw in 1955: "I'm working hard all the time and have several exhibitions at the moment and many coming up—I now only do fabric designs on special request."[22] Indeed from then on, at the age of seventy, Sonia continued to paint with relentless vigor and joie de vivre, for nearly twenty-five more years. She remained a versatile artist: in addition to her painting, she made numerous lithographs, designed books, tapestries (Metz & Co exhibited her latest designs in 1967), rugs, mosaics, playing cards, and occasionally fabrics and scarves, such as those she designed for Metz's longstanding associate Liberty's of London (FIGS. 9, 12, 13, 14).[23]

FIG. 14. Scarf. Produced by Liberty's of London. France, ca. 1967. Printed silk voile. Private collection

FIG. 15. Gouache. France, 1938. Watercolor, gouache, and pencil on paper. Private collection

1938   Sonia Delaunay

NOTES

PAGE 162

1 In her book *Atelier Simultané di Sonia Delaunay 1923–1934* (Milan: Fabbri Editori, 1984), Annette Malochet made a very informative and comprehensive study of Delaunay's *Livres noirs*. However, she attributed a number of designs to the time of the Atelier Simultané which, according to the design numbers, clearly date from the 1940s and 1950s. New versions of this book were made in 2003 for the Musée de Lodève, France, and in 2006 for the Museo Villa dei Cedri, Bellinzona, Switzerland.

2 The *Livres noirs* are currently in a private collection.

PAGE 169

3 For instance, design nos. 7, 35, 42, 43, 47, 188, 189, 205, 222bis, 226bis, 279, 294, 503, 549, 599, 642, 649, 765, 889a, 890f, 891gr, 892bis, 903. Also, in the 1940s and 1950s, Metz & Co reissued some older designs.

4 When Delaunay started her atelier in 1924, she used *graveurs* (woodcarvers) for the woodblocks needed for printing on silk. She lists two companies, Oudé and Ferret, which both did her printing as well. Many of the woodblocks used by Ferret were rediscovered some years ago. Delaunay also did the carving herself, as she was technically very involved and liked to be in control of the process of her designs. Other names listed are Cornier and Tissus d'Art, on the rue de Levis.

5 Companies to which she sold her designs from *Livre noir* I were Godau-Guillaume-Arnaut, of 12, rue Sainte Anne in Paris, La Manufacture des Velours et Peluches in Lyon, Hickert et fils, Carrier, and Prévost Lyon. There were two important American clients: Eagle, in 1925; and Foreman Foremort Fabrics Corporation of 389 Fifth Avenue, New York, in 1928. Except for what was made in her atelier and bore a label of Maison Delaunay, she is never mentioned as the designer by companies that bought her fabric designs. Also, in America, she remained anonymous at that time.

PAGE 171

6 In 1918, Delaunay designed costumes for Sergei Diaghilev's revival production of the ballet *Cléopâtre* in London.

7 Sonia Delaunay, *Compositions, Couleurs, Idées* (Moreau, 1930).

8 *Livre noir* IX also lists names as Vogelman, Porcher & Zelpen, B. Mann, Riefe, de Roze, Lambert, Logan Cheney, McGrimes, Menke Kaufmann, and Lievin, firms that bought small amounts of her designs. Metz & Co was clearly her most important partner.

9 Also in 1938, she made a "summary of account with Metz": Journal, October 25, 1938: *"Après le déjeuner rapporte dans le cahier ouvert à ce sujet le resumé de comptes avec Metz arreté l´année dernière en septembre. 25.000 Fr. avance."* ("After lunch, I made in the notebook started for this purpose a summary of accounts for Metz ending in September of last year. 25,000 francs advanced.")

10 *Voyages lointains* and *Portugal* for the Palais de Chemin de Fer, and the large panels *L'Hélice, Le Moteur*, and the *Tableau de Bord* for the Palais de l'Air, in Paris.

11 Felix Aublet (1903–1978) French architect, designer, and painter. In 1935, Robert and Sonia worked in his office as colorist and designer. In 1936, Aublet set up with Robert a limited company, Art et Lumière, to prepare for the 1937 Expo.

PAGE 174

12 After Robert's death, Sonia started only gradually to paint again in 1942. On Aug. 9, 1943, she noted in her journal, *"Je me suis mise à travailler et ai commencé une gouache. J'aimerais lier le principe des tissus avec la peinture, ce que me conseillait toujours Robert."* ("I got to work and started on a gouache. I would like to connect the principles of fabrics with painting, which Robert always advised me to do.")

13 Journal, June 15, 1942: *"Sortie du panier no.2 du garde meuble les tissus Metz."*

14 Sonia got Hans Arp to take some of these paintings into Switzerland to be sold to provide her with some much needed cash. See Bernier & Schneider-Maunoury, *R. et S. Delaunay, Naissance de l'art abstrait* (Lattès, 1995): 252.

15 Journal, April 2, 1942. Maison Gonnet was the manufacturer for Robert Perrier.

16 Journal, April 17, 1942: *"Vendu à Perrier dessins pour tissus: 100-131 (31 à 200fr = 6200 fr) 28 Impressions, 3 tissages."*

17 Journal, October 7, 1945: *"Ajouté à l'inventaire dessins no 4501, 4502, 4503, 4504, 4505, 4506 serie H."*

18 Journal, June 9, 1946: *"Fait 13 Dessins de tissus 4601–4613…. Je me suis mise à travailler. Fait des dessins de tissus pour Metz en écoutant les nouvelles sportives à la radio. C'est l'émission que je préfère. Elle est vivante et pas idiote. Fait 13 dessins qui sont sortis très facilement."*

PAGE 183

19 Letter H. de Leeuw to Sonia Delaunay, February 7, 1950, and Delaunay's journal.

20 See Malochet, *Sonia Delaunay, l'Atelier Simultané, 1923–1934*, Musée de Lodéve: Mazzota, 2003 pp. 143–46.

21 See Malochet/Bianchi, *Sonia Delaunay, l'Atelier Simultané, 1923–1934* (Bellinzona: Skira, 2006): 76, 80.

22 *"Je travaille toujours beaucoup et ai plusieurs expositions en ce moment et beaucoup d'autres en vue — Des dessins de tissus je ne fais que sur commande."* Delaunay letter to H. de Leeuw, January 19, 1955.

23 For instance, scarves in 1969. Heim reissued two older "rayures" designs, which Sonia had revised in 1961 (Delaunay letter to H. de Leeuw, March 19, 1961). The English company Ascher reedited some early Delaunay designs in 1966 (now in the collection of the V&A Museum, London); see Journal, July 4, 1966. Artcurial in Paris reissued many of Sonia's designs in the late 1970s and 1980s, but the result was not comparable in quality to her original work.

BIBLIOGRAPHY

BOOKS AND FOLIOS WITH PRINTS BY SONIA DELAUNAY

10 Origin: album of 10 original lithographs by Arp, Bill, Delaunay, Domela, Kandinsky, Leuppi, Lohse, Magnelli, Taeuber-Arp, and Vantongerloo. Zurich: Allianz-Verlag, 1942.

Aux Nourritures Terrestres. Ten lithographed plates with collaboration of Sonia Delaunay, Jean Arp, Alberto Magnelli, and Sophie Tauber-Arp. Grasse, 1942.

Cendrars, Blaise. *La Prose du Transsibérien et de la Petite Jehanne de France.* Paris: Hommes Nouveaux, 1913.

Damase, Jacques, ed. *Robes poèmes.* Poems written for Sonia Delaunay by Cendrars, Apollinaire, Tzara, Delteil, and others. Milan: Edizioni del Naviglio, 1969.

———, ed. *Sonia Delaunay: Dessins noirs et blancs.* Paris: Artcurial, 1978.

———, ed. *Sonia Delaunay: Robes et gouaches simultanées, 1925 - L'Art et le corps rythmes – couleurs en mouvement.* Brussels: Jacques Damase Editeur, 1974.

———, ed. *Sonia Delaunay: Rythmes et couleurs.* Paris: Hermann, 1971. (English ed. *Sonia Delaunay: Rhythms and Colors.* Greenwich, CT, and London: New York Graphic Society and Thames & Hudson, 1972).

Delaunay, Sonia. *Alphabet,* English ed. New York: Thomas Y. Crowell, 1972.

———. *Compositions, couleurs, idées.* Paris: Editions d'Art Charles Moreau, 1930.

———. *Six planches gravées à l'eau forte.* Milan: Galerie Schwartz, 1966.

Lhote, André, ed. *Sonia Delaunay: Ses peintures, ses objets, ses tissus simultanés, ses modes.* Paris: Librairie des Arts Décoratifs, 1925.

Poésie de mots, poésie de couleurs. Poems by Rimbaud, Tzara, Soupault, Cendrars, Delteil, and Mallarmé. With six pochoir prints by Sonia Delaunay. Paris: Éditions Denise René, 1962.

Rimbaud, Arthur. *Les Illuminations.* With 15 pochoir prints by Sonia Delaunay. Paris: Atelier-Galerie Jack Renaud, 1973.

Tzara, Tristan. *Juste présent.* With 6 etchings by Sonia Delaunay. France: Rose des vents, 1961.

———. *Le Cœur à gaz,* by Tristan Tzara, with lithographs after the 1923 costumes by Sonia Delaunay. Paris: G.L.M, 1946.

———. *Le fruit permis: Poèmes. Avec 4 compositions au pochoir de Sonia Delaunay.* Paris: Caractères, 1956.

WRITINGS BY SONIA DELAUNAY

Cohen, Arthur A., ed. *The New Art of Color: the Writings of Robert and Sonia Delaunay.* New York: Viking Press, 1978.

———. "Les Artistes et l'avenir de la mode." In *Revue de Jacques Heim* no. 3 (September 1932). Reprinted in Radu Stern, *Against Fashion: Clothing as Art 1850–1930.* Cambridge, MA, and London: MIT Press, 2004): 186.

———. "L'influence de la peinture sur la mode." In *Bulletin des Etudes Philosophiques et Scientifiques pour l'examen des tendances nouvelles (Paris, 1927).* Reprinted in Stern, 183–85.

———. *Nous irons jusqu'au soleil.* Paris: Editions Robert Laffont, 1978.

———. "Robert et Sonia Delaunay, Art et mouvement, la couleur dansée." In *Aujourd'hui, art et architecture (Boulogne-sur-Seine),* vol. 3 no. 17, (May 1958): 7–9.

Delaunay, Sonia. *Tapis et tissus, présenté par Sonia Delaunay.* Series: L'Art international d'aujourd'hui, no. 15. Paris: Editions d'Art Charles Moreau, 1929.

WRITINGS ABOUT SONIA DELAUNAY

Albritton, Ann Hill. *Sonia Delaunay-Terk: The Zenith Years, 1906–1914.* Ph.D. dissertation submitted to the City University of New York, 1997.

Baron, Stanley, in collaboration with Jacques Damase. *Sonia Delaunay: The Life of an Artist.* New York and London: Harry N. Abrams and Thames & Hudson, 1995.

Bernier, Georges, and Monique Schneider-Maunoury. *Robert et Sonia Delaunay: Naissance de l'art abstrait.* Paris: J–C. Lattès, 1995.

Cohen, Arthur A. *Sonia Delaunay.* New York: Harry N. Abrams, 1975.

Damase, Jacques, ed. *Sonia Delaunay: Fashion and Fabrics* (translated from the French by Shaun Whiteside and Stanley Brown). New York: Harry N. Abrams, 1991.

———. *Sonia Delaunay: Her Art and Fashion.* New York: George Braziller, 1985.

Desanti, Dominique. *Sonia Delaunay: Magique magicienne.* Paris: Editions Ramsay, 1988.

Dorival, Bernard. *Sonia Delaunay: sa vie, son œuvre 1885–1979.* Paris: Éditions Jacques Damase, 1980.

Giordano, Marina. *Sonia Delaunay: La Danza del colore.* Milan: Selene, 2003.

Kuthy, Sandor. *Sonia & Robert Delaunay: Künstlerpaare, Künstlerfreunde/Dialogue d'artistes, résonances.* Stuttgard: Gerd Hatje, 1991.

Madsen, Axel. *Sonia Delaunay: Artist of the Lost Generation.* New York: McGraw-Hill, 1989.

Malochet, Annette. *Atelier simultané di Sonia Delaunay 1923–34.* Milan: Fabbri, 1984.

Morano, Elizabeth, with foreword by Diana Vreeland. *Sonia Delaunay: Art into Fashion.* New York: George Braziller, 1986.

Nemser, Cindy. "Sonia Delaunay." In *Art Talk: Conversations with 12 Women Artists* (New York: Scribner, 1975): 34–51.

Rousseau, Pascal. *La Aventura simultànea: Sonia y Robert Delaunay en Barcelona.* Barcelona: Universitat de Barcelona, 1995.

EXHIBITION CATALOGUES

Brentjes, Yvonne. *Sonia Delaunay: Dessins.* Tilburg: Nederlands Texteilmuseum, 1988.

Buckberrough, Sherry A. *Sonia Delaunay, a Retrospective.* Buffalo: Albright-Knox Art Gallery, 1980.

Castro, Jan Garden. *Sonia Delaunay: La Moderne,* exhibition held at Urawa Art Museum, January 5–March 10, 2002, and three other museums through September 8, 2002. Japan: Yomiuri Shimbun, Japan Association of Art Museums, Art Impressions, 2002.

Damase, Jacques, and Edouard Mustelier. *Sonia Delaunay.* Paris: Galerie de Varenne, 1971.

Dupuits, Petra. *Sonia Delaunay: Metz est venu.* Amsterdam: Stedelijk Museum, 1992.

Hülsewig-Johnen, Jutta, ed. *Sonia Delaunay: Welt der Kunst.* Bielefeld, Germany: Kunsthalle Bielefeld, 2008.

Léal, Brigitte. *La donation Sonia et Charles Delaunay dans les collections du Centre Georges Pompidou, Musée national d'art moderne,* October 1, 2003–January 5, 2004. Paris: Centre Pompidou, 2003.

Malochet, Annette, and Matteo Bianchi. *Sonia Delaunay: Atelier simultané,* April 12–June 11, 2006. Milan: Skira; Bellizona, Switzerland: Museo villa dei Cedri, 2006.

Oliva, Achille Bonito, and Annette Malochet. *Sonia Delaunay: Atelier Simultané 1923–34,* exhibition at Galleria Bevilacqua La Masa, Venice. Milan: Mazzotta, 2002.

Robert y Sonia Delaunay: Exposición organizada en asociación con el Musée National d'Art Moderne, Centre Georges Pompidou: Barcelona: Museu Picasso y Museu Tèxtil i d'Indumentària, October 20, 2000–January 21, 2001. Carroggio: Institut de Cultura, 2000.

Sonia Delaunay: Dissenys tèxtils holandesos. Barcelona: Fundació La Caixa, 1995.

Sonia Delaunay: Etoffes imprimées des années folles. Mulhouse: Musée de l'impression sur Etoffes de Mulhouse, 1971.

Sonia Delaunay: Retrospektivausstellung zum 90/Retrospective on the Occasion of Her 90th birthday, Ausstellung vorn 4 november bis 31 dezember 1975. Cologne: Galerie Gmurzynska, 1975.

Sonia Delaunay: Rhythmes et couleurs, New York, NY, October–December 1986; Bremen, February–April 1987. New York: Helen Serger/La Boétie; Bremen: Kunsthandel Wolfgang Werner KG, 1986.

Sonia Delaunay: Works of the Teens and Twenties. New York: Leonard Cohen Galleries, 1995.

Timmer, Petra. *Sonia Delaunay, Tecidos Simultâneos.* Porto: Museu Soares dos Reis, Dec 13, 2001–February 24, 2002.

EXHIBITION CHECKLIST

UNLESS OTHERWISE NOTED, ALL WORKS ARE DESIGNED BY SONIA DELAUNAY (FRENCH, BORN RUSSIA, 1885–1979). NUMBERS IN PARENTHESES AT THE END OF THE ENTRIES INDICATE THE PAGE ON WHICH THE IMAGE OF THE OBJECT APPEARS IN THIS PUBLICATION.

Dress. France, 1925–28. Printed silk satin with metallic embroidery. Musée de la Mode de la Ville de Paris, Galliera, GAL 1970.58.31 (15)

Prospectus La Prose du Transsibérien. France, 1913. Gouache, pochoir (recto/verso), 9.2 x 32 cm (3 ¾ x 13 ½ in.). Collection of Antoine Blanchette (14)

De la loi du contraste simultané des couleurs, et de l'assortiment des objets colorés, considéré d'après cette loi. Written by Michel Eugène Chevreul (French, 1786–1889). Published by Imprimerie Nationale. France, 1889. Leather, paper, ink, color engraving, 7 x 26.4 x 33.7 cm (2 ¾ x 10 ⅜ x 13 ¼ in.). Smithsonian Institution Libraries, QND1280.C52 1889 (26)

Robe-poème pour Tzara (Dress-poem for Tzara). France, 1923. Watercolor on paper, 31.1 x 19.3 cm (12 ¼ x 7 ⅝ in.). Private Collection (28)

Robe poème no. 1329. France, 1923. Watercolor, gouache, and pencil on paper, 36.9 x 23.7 cm (14 ½ x 9 ⅜ in.). Museum of Modern Art, New York, 301.1980 Purchase (30)

Robe poème no. 688. France, 1922. Watercolor, gouache, and pencil on paper. 31.2 x 23.8 cm (12 ¼ x 9 ⅜ in.). Museum of Modern Art, New York 303.1980 Purchase (28)

Cover for La Prose du Transsibérien et de la petite Jehanne de France. France, 1913. Oil on leather, 23.2 x 19.7 cm (9 ⅛ x 7 ¾ in.). Courtesy of Barry Friedman and Patricia Pastor (13)

La Prose du Transsibérien et de la petite Jehanne de France. Text by Blaise Cendrars (Frédéric-Louis Sauser, French born Switzerland, 1886–1961). Illustrated by Sonia Delaunay. Published by Éditions des Hommes Nouveaux. Paris, France, 1913. Illustrated book with pochoir, composition, 207.4 x 36.2 cm (78 ⅜ in. x 14 ¼ in.). Museum of Modern Art, New York 133.1951 A-B (14)

Gouache. France, 1938. Watercolor, gouache, and pencil on paper, 40.5 x 25.5 cm (16 x 10 in.). Private Collection (185)

Rythme Coloré. France, 1946. Oil on canvas, 175.3 x 149.9 cm (69 x 59 in.). Private Collection (24)

Rythme No. 5. France, 1939. Gouache on paper, 27.3 x 23 cm (10 ¾ x 9 ⅛ in.). Private Collection (8)

Album no. 1, no. 999. France, 1916. Encaustic on paper, 23.9 x 23.6 cm (9 ½ x 9 ⅜ in.). Private Collection (13)

Autoportrait no. 962 (self-portrait for the Stockholm catalogue). France, 1916. Encaustic on paper, 31.9 x 31.2 cm (12 ⅝ x 12 ⅜ in.). Private Collection (26)

Sonia Delaunay and two models in Robert Delaunay's studio, 1924. Photographic reproduction. Bibliothèque Nationale de France, Paris (36–37)

Folio: Compositions, Couleurs, Idées. Published by Editions d'Art Charles Moreau. France, 1930. Pochoir on paper, 32 x 24.5 cm (12 ⅝ x 9 ⅝ in.). Private Collection

Still photo from the film *Le P'tit Parigot.* Written by Paul Cartoux. Directed by René Le Somptier. France, 1926. Photographic reproduction. Collection of Antoine Blanchette (40)

Pyjama for Tristan Tzara. France, 1923. Watercolor and pencil on paper, 31 x 22.8 cm (12 ¼ x 9 in.). Museum of Modern Art, New York, The Joan and Lester Avnet Collection 30.1978 (29)

Robe poème no. 1328. France, 1923. Watercolor, gouache, and pencil on paper, 35.2 x 30.7 cm (13 ⅞ x 12 ⅛ in.). Museum of Modern Art, New York, 304.1980 Purchase (31)

ATELIER SIMULTANÉ

Portrait of Sonia Delaunay. Photographed by Florence Henri (American, 1893–1982). France, 1931. Gelatin silver print, 29.2 x 23.5 cm (11 ½ x 9 ¼ in.). Courtesy of Barry Friedman and Patricia Pastor (FRONT FLAP)

Model no. 200, Feuilles d'automne (Autumn Leaves) **embroidered panel made from parts of a coat.** France, 1924. Wool embroidery on cotton canvas, 134 x 191 cm (53 x 75 ½ in.). Les Arts Décoratifs, Paris, UF65-10-8 (27)

Portrait of Nancy Cunard. France, 1924. China crayon on paper, 38.7 x 28.6 cm (15 ¼ x 11 ¼ in.). Courtesy of Barry Friedman and Patricia Pastor (41)

Coat made for Gloria Swanson. France, 1923–24. Wool embroidery on cotton canvas. Private Collection (38–39)

Shawl. France, 1925–30. Knitted wool. Les Arts Décoratifs, Paris, 47694 (72)

Tissu simultané (Simultaneous textile) no. 193. France, 1927. Block-printed on silk, wool jersey, cotton, 50 x 19 cm (19 ¾ x 7 ½ in.), 39.5 x 23 cm (15 ⅝ x 9 ⅛ in.), 58 x 37 cm (22 ⅞ x 14 ⅝ in.). Musée de l'Impression sur Étoffes, Mulhouse, 980.554.4,6,16 (56–57)

Embroidery samples no. 9. France, 1928. Wool embroidery on cotton canvas, 25 x 24 cm (9 ⅞ x 9 ½ in.). Les Arts Décoratifs, Paris, 47681 A-B

Tissu simultané. France, 1929. Block-printed silk crêpe de chine, 37 x 49.5 cm (14 ⅝ x 19 ½ in.). Musée de l'Impression sur Étoffes, Mulhouse, 980.611.8 (57)

Embroidery sample for a purse. France, ca. 1926. Silk embroidery on silk crêpe de chine, 36 x 43 cm (14 ¼ x 17 in.). Les Arts Décoratifs, Paris, 47724

Tissu simultané. France, 1928. Block-printed silk crêpe de chine, 34 x 22 cm (13 ⅜ x 8 ¾ in.). Musée de l'Impression sur Étoffes, Mulhouse, 980.585.6 (2)

Tissu simultané. France, 1924–25. Block-printed on silk velvet, silk crêpe de chine, 28 x 21 cm (11 x 8 ¼ in.), 27 x 17 cm (10 ⅝ x 6 ¾ in.). Musée de l'Impression sur Étoffes, Mulhouse, 980.563BIS.5,8 (74–75)

Tissu simultané no. 145. France, 1926. Block-printed silk crêpe de chine, 51.5 x 26 cm (20 ¼ x 10 ¼ in.), 51 x 25 cm (20 ⅛ x 9 ⅞ in.). Musée de l'Impression sur Étoffes, Mulhouse, 980.539.2, 4 (76–77)

Siégel showroom with mannequin designed by René Herbst and textile designed by Sonia Delaunay, ca. 1926. Photographed by Thérèse Bonney. Photographic reproduction. Smithsonian Institution Libraries, V-977 MAN 031 (21)

Driving caps. France, 1924–28. Silk and wool embroidery on cotton canvas. Musée de la Mode de la Ville de Paris, Galliera, GAL 1971.24.3 C,D (53)

Embroidery samples no. 18. France, 1924. Wool embroidery on cotton canvas. (A) 23 x 13 cm (9 ⅛ x 5 ⅛ in.); (B) 27.5 x 9.8 cm (10 ⅞ x 3 ⅞ in.); (C) 29.8 x 14.2 cm (11 ¾ x 5 ⅝ in.); (D) 30 x 12 cm (11 ⅞ x 4 ¾ in.); (E) 27.5 x 13.5 cm (10 ⅞ x 5 ⅜ in.); (F) 29.5 x 13 cm (11 ⅝ x 5 ⅛ in.); (G) 31.8 x 16.5 cm (12 ½ x 6 ½ in.). Les Arts Décoratifs, Paris, 47719 A-G

Model wearing Sonia Delaunay coat, ca. 1925. Bibliothèque Nationale de France, Paris (54)

Two models wearing Sonia Delaunay beachwear, 1928. 23.5 x 17.1 cm (9 ¼ x 6 ¾ in.). Private Collection (57–58)

Skirt, Tissu simultané no. 186. France, ca. 1926. Block-printed wool jersey. Musée de l'Impression sur Étoffes, Mulhouse, 980.549.11 (60)

Tissu simultané no. 186. France, 1926. Block-printed cotton, 29 x 19.5 cm (11 ½ x 7 ¾ in.), 58 x 30 cm (22 ⅞ x 11 ⅞ in.). Musée de l'Impression sur Étoffes, Mulhouse, 980.549.17, 18 (59)

Eyre de Lanux in Sonia Delaunay coat, ca. 1928. Photograph. 28 x 20.1 cm (11 x 8 ½ in.). Collection of Antoine Blanchette (41)

Tissu simultané no. 204. Printed by Ferret. France, 1927. Block-printed silk crêpe de chine, (A) 44 x 26.5 cm (17 ⅜ x 10 ½ in.), (B) 54 x 22.5 cm (21 ¼ x 8 ⅞ in.). Les Arts Décoratifs, Paris, 40412 A-B (67)

Projet de tissu simultané (Design for Simultaneous Textile). France, 1927. Watercolor on paper, 32.7 x 25.6 cm (12 ⅞ x 10 ⅛ in.). Les Arts Décoratifs, Paris, 40411 (66)

Projet de tissu simultané no. 204. France, 1927. Watercolor on paper, 33.3 x 26.8 cm (13 ⅛ x 10 ⅝ in.). Les Arts Décoratifs, Paris, 40410 (67)

Les Arts Plastiques (The Plastic Arts) no. 2. Cover illustration by Sonia Delaunay. France, 1925. Block-printed on paper, 24.8 x 15.9 cm (9 ¾ x 6 ¼ in.). Collection of Antoine Blanchette (19)

Projet de tissu simultané no. 34. France, 1924. Watercolor on paper, 52 x 33.4 cm (20 ½ x 13 ¼ in.). Les Arts Décoratifs, Paris, 40397 (18)

Scarf, tissu simultané no. 186. France, 1926. Block-printed silk, 148 x 45 cm (58 ¼ x 17 ¾ in.). Private Collection (61)

Projet de tissu simultané no. 186. France, 1926. Watercolor on paper, 31 x 47 cm (12 ¼ x 18 ½ in.), Les Arts Décoratifs, Paris, 40406 (61)

Tissu simultané no. 59. France, 1924. Block-printed silk velvet, 78.5 x 27 cm (30 ⅞ x 10 ⅝ in.). Musée de l'Impression sur Étoffes, Mulhouse, 980.527.5

Tissu simultané. France, 1924–25. Block-printed cotton velveteen, 78 x 26 cm (30 ¾ x 10 ¼ in.). Musée de l'Impression sur Étoffes, Mulhouse, 980.507.1 (80–81)

Tissu simultané fabric samples. France, 1926. Block-printed silk crêpe de chine, 53.3 x 32.5 cm (21 ⅛ x 12 ⅞ in.). Musée de l'Impression sur Étoffes, Mulhouse, 980.513.1-4 (82)

Embroidery sample. France, ca. 1924. Silk and metal embroidery on silk crêpe georgette, 26 x 22 cm (10 ¼ x 8 ¾ in.). Les Arts Décoratifs, Paris, 47723 C

Embroidery sample. France, ca. 1927. Mercerized cotton and metallic embroidery on cotton canvas, 24 x 13 cm (9 ½ x 5 ⅛ in.). Les Arts Décoratifs, Paris, 47723 B

Embroidery sample. France, ca. 1927. Cotton embroidery on cotton canvas, 18 x 11 cm (7 ⅛ x 4 ⅜ in.). Les Arts Décoratifs, Paris, 47723 A

Embroidery samples no. 168. France, 1927. Cotton and wool embroidery on cotton canvas, 26 x 23 cm (10 ¼ x 9 ⅛ in.). Les Arts Décoratifs, Paris, 47686 A-D

Tissu simultané no. 205 design card and fabric sample. France, 1927. Produced by Metz & Co, 1934. Gouache, ink, and pencil on paper; block-printed cotton, 21.4 x 24.2 cm (8 ½ x 9 ½ in.), 48 x 54.5 cm (18 ⅞ x 21 ½ in.). Private Collection (44–45)

Tissu simultané no. 205. France, 1927. Block-printed on cotton velveteen, cotton, 37.5 x 22 cm (14 ¾ x 8 ¾ in.), 58 x 20 cm (22 ⅞ x 7 ⅞ in.), 16 x 16 cm (6 ⅜ x 6 ⅜ in.). Musée de l'Impression sur Étoffes, Mulhouse, 980.563.25, 56, 69 (65, 201)

Embroidery samples no. 186. France, 1927. Wool embroidery on cotton canvas, 22 x 26 cm (8 ¾ x 10 ¼ in.). Les Arts Décoratifs, Paris, 47688 A-D

Embroidery samples no. 162. France, 1927. Mercerized cotton embroidery on cotton canvas, 26 x 23 cm (10 ¼ x 9 ⅛ in.). Les Arts Décoratifs, Paris, 47685 A-D

Fabric fragment. France, ca. 1927. Silk embroidery on wool jersey, 56 x 50 cm (22 ⅛ x 19 ¾ in.). Les Arts Décoratifs, Paris, 47726

Tissu simultané no. 60. France, 1924. Block-printed cotton velveteen, 33 x 24 cm (13 x 9 ½ in.). Musée de l'Impression sur Étoffes, Mulhouse, 980.528.2 (6)

Tissu simultané no. 266. France, ca. 1928. Block-printed silk, 49 x 24 cm (19 ⅜ x 9 ½ in.). Musée de l'Impression sur Étoffes, Mulhouse, 980.567.5 (73)

Tissu simultané. France, 1924–25. Block-printed cotton, 61.5 x 24.5 cm (25 ¼ x 9 ⅝ in.). Musée de l'Impression sur Étoffes, Mulhouse, 980.501.2 (69)

Tissu simultané no. 46. France, 1924–25. Block-printed cotton velveteen, 71 x 33 cm (28 x 13 in.). Musée de l'Impression sur Étoffes, Mulhouse, 980.614.2 (80–81)

Tissu simultané no. 166. France, 1926. Block-printed cotton, 59 x 29 cm (23 ¼ x 11 ½ in.). Musée de l'Impression sur Étoffes, Mulhouse, 980.503.4 (69)

Two models in Sonia Delaunay's boulevard Malesherbes studio, 1925. Photographed by Germaine Krull. Photographic reproduction. Bibliothèque Nationale de France, Paris (68)

Model wearing Sonia Delaunay pyjama at the Exposition Internationale des Arts Décoratifs, Paris, in an interior designed by Pierre Chareau, 1925. Photographic reproduction. Private Collection (17)

Model wearing Sonia Delaunay dress, ca. 1927. Photographic reproduction. Bibliothèque Nationale de France, Paris (71)

Skirt panel, Tissu simultané no. 11. France, 1924. Block-printed silk crêpe de chine, 51 x 94 cm (20 ⅛ x 37 in.). Musée de l'Impression sur Étoffes, Mulhouse, 980.518.3 (70)

Tissu simultané no. 7. France, 1924–25. Block-printed silk chiffon with silk embroidery and glass beads, 76.2 x 45.7 cm (30 x 18 in.). Musée de l'Impression sur Étoffes, Mulhouse, 980.516.5 (73)

Projet de tissu simultané no. 6. France, 1924. Watercolor on paper, 35 x 51 cm (13 ¾ x 20 ⅛ in.). Les Arts Décoratifs, Paris, 40393 (12)

Projet de tissu simultané no. 25. France, 1924. Watercolor on paper, 35 x 51 cm (13 ¾ x 20 ⅛ in.). Les Arts Décoratifs, Paris, 40394 (83)

Bathing suit (tunic). France, 1924–25. Silk embroidery on wool jersey. Musée de l'Impression sur Étoffes, Mulhouse, 980.629.1 (63)

Bathing suit (tunic and shorts), tissu simultané no. 205. France, 1927. Block-printed cotton. Musée de l'Impression sur Étoffes, Mulhouse, 980.621.1,2 (63)

Model wearing Sonia Delaunay swimsuit, 1929. Photographed by Luigi Diaz for Presse Paris. Photographic reproduction. Bibliothèque Nationale de France, Paris (62)

Bathing suit. France, ca. 1928. Knitted wool. Musée de la Mode de la Ville de Paris, Galliera, GAL 1971.24.7 (63)

Three models wearing Sonia Delaunay coats in the Bois de Boulogne, ca. 1927. Photographic reproduction. Bibliothèque Nationale de France, Paris (55)

Two models wearing Sonia Delaunay fashions beside a Citroën B12 decorated by the artist, 1925. Photographic reproduction. Bibliothèque Nationale de France, Paris (19)

*Projet de tissu simultané
no. 30.* France, 1924.
Watercolor on paper,
48 × 32 cm (18 ⅞ × 12 ⅝ in.).
Les Arts Décoratifs, Paris,
40395 (78)

*Projet de tissu simultané
no. 33.* France, 1924.
Watercolor on paper,
47 × 33.8 cm (18 ½ × 13 ⅜ in.).
Les Arts Décoratifs, Paris,
40396 (84)

Hat and scarf. France,
1923. Block-printed cotton
with silk tassels. Musée de
l'Impression sur Étoffes,
Mulhouse, 980.620.1,2 (64)

Purse. France, 1923. Block-
printed cotton with silk
tassel, 17 × 29 cm (6 ¾ ×
11 ½ in.). Les Arts Décoratifs,
Paris, 47704

Tissu simultané. France,
ca. 1924. Block-printed silk
crêpe de chine, 81 × 51 cm
(31 ⅞ × 20 ⅛ in.). Musée de
l'Impression sur Étoffes,
Mulhouse, 980.514.1 (85)

**Scarf, Tissu simultané
no. 70.** Printed by Ferret.
France, 1924. Block-printed
silk crêpe de chine, 140 × 47 cm
(55 ⅛ × 18 ½ in.). Les Arts
Décoratifs, Paris, 40402 (34)

**Scarf, Tissu simultané
no. 14.** France, 1924–25.
Block-printed cotton, 96 ×
22 cm (37 ⅞ × 8 ¾ in.). Musée
de l'Impression sur Étoffes,
Mulhouse, 980.619.1 (84)

Scarf. France, 1924–25.
Wool reverse appliqué, 101 ×
30 cm (39 ¾ × 11 ⅞ in.). Musée
de l'Impression sur Étoffes,
Mulhouse, 980.634.1 (34)

Scarf. France, 1924–25.
Woven wool, 120 × 39 cm
(47 ¼ × 15 ⅜ in.). Musée de
l'Impression sur Étoffes,
Mulhouse, 980.638.1 (35)

Boutique Simultané, in
René Herbst, *Devantures,
vitrines, installation de
magasins à l'exposition
internationale des arts
décoratifs*, plate 18. Paris,
France, 1925. Photographic
reproduction. Smithsonian
Institution Libraries
FNA6225.H4Z (32)

*Composition abstracte
diagonale no. 1733.* France,
1925. Gouache on paper,
47 × 31.5 cm (18 ½ × 12 ⅜ in.).
Private Collection (79)

METZ & CO

*Design for Metz & Co
Delivery Car.* Bart van der
Leck (Dutch, 1876–1958).
The Netherlands, 1930.
Gouache and pencil on
tracing paper, 80 × 60 cm
(31 ½ × 23 ⅝ in.). Private
Collection (114)

Design 1318. France, 1934.
Design cards: gouache, ink,
and pencil on paper,
21 × 23.8 cm (8 ¼ × 9 ⅜ in.),
21.2 × 23.9 cm (8 ⅜ × 9 ½ in.);
fabric book: gouache, ink,
and pencil on paper with
fabric swatches, 45 × 35 cm
(17 ¾ × 13 ¾ in.). Private
Collection (46–47)

**Packaging for Metz & Co/
Amsterdam /Den Haag.**
Designed by Bart van der
Leck. The Netherlands, 1952.
Gift bags: black and red ink
on off-white paper, screen-
printed, 31 × 13 × 0.6 cm (12 ¼ ×
5 ⅛ × ¼ in.), 23.5 × 23.5 ×
1 cm (9 ¼ × 9 ¼ × ⅜ in.); box:
black and red ink on brown
cardboard, screen-printed,
5.4 × 39.4 × 29.2 cm (2 ⅛ ×
15 ½ × 11 ½ in.). Cooper-Hewitt,
National Design Museum,
Smithsonian Institution, 1994-
63-2,4,5. Gift of Ms. June Braun
and Mr. Robert Leibowits (114)

Metz & Co logo.
Designed by Gerrit Rietveld
(Dutch, 1888–1964).
The Netherlands, ca. 1938.
Pencil and ink on tracing
paper, 19 × 24.2 cm (7 ½ ×
9 ½ in.) Private Collection (114)

**Exhibition of Sonia Delaunay
fabrics in the Rietveld cupola
of Metz & Co, Amsterdam,
the Netherlands, 1934.**
Photographic reproduction.
Private Collection (123)

Metz & Co. Amsterdam,
the Netherlands, ca. 1960.
Photographic reproduction.
Private Collection (106)

**Metz & Co storefront with
windows designed by Gerrit
Rietveld, Amsterdam,
the Netherlands, ca. 1949.**
Photographic reproduction.
Private Collection (115)

**Metz & Co window display
designed by Gerrit Rietveld,
with Bart van der Leck rug,
Burkhalter chair, Djo
Bourgeois table, the Hague,
the Netherlands, 1934.**
Photographic reproduction.
Private Collection

**Exhibition of Rietveld
furniture at Metz
"Meubelhuis" (furniture
store), Amsterdam,
the Netherlands, ca. 1940.**
Photographic reproduction.
Private Collection

Design 957. France, 1929.
Produced by Metz & Co,
1930. Working drawing:
gouache on tracing paper,
17 × 25 cm (9 ⅞ × 6 ¾ in.);
textile design: gouache, ink,
and pencil on paper, 26.5 ×
21 cm (10 ½ × 8 ¼ in.); design
card: gouache, ink, and
pencil on paper, with fabric
swatch, 21.3 × 24 cm (8 ⅜ ×
9 ½ in.); 5 fabric samples:
block-printed silk, 14.5 ×
13 cm (5 ¾ × 5 ⅛ in.), 11.5 ×
14.5 cm (4 ½ × 5 ¾ in.), 11.5 ×
14.5 cm (4 ½ × 5 ¾ in.), 10.5 ×
14.5 cm (4 ⅛ × 5 ¾ in.), 14.5 ×
13 cm (5 ¾ × 5 ⅛ in.). Private
Collection (124–25)

Design 226 bis.
France, 1928. Produced by
Metz & Co, 1930. Textile
design: gouache, ink, and
pencil on paper, 26.9 ×
20.9 cm (10 ⅝ × 8 ¼ in.);
design card: gouache, ink,
and pencil on paper, 21.4 ×
24 cm (8 ½ × 9 ½ in.); 6 fabric
samples: printed silk,
11 × 7 cm (4 ⅜ × 2 ¾ in.),
13 × 5.5 cm (5 ⅛ × 2 ¼ in.),
13 × 9 cm (5 ⅛ × 3 ⅝ in.),
14 × 7.5 cm (5 ½ × 3 in.),
13 × 6 cm (5 ⅛ × 2 ⅜ in.),
13 × 15 cm (5 ⅛ × 5 ⅞ in.).
Private Collection (88–91)

Design 945. France, 1929. Produced by Metz & Co, 1930. Textile design: gouache, ink, and pencil on paper, 26.9 × 20.9 cm (10 ⅝ × 8 ¼ in.); design card: gouache, ink, and pencil on paper, with silk swatch, 24.1 × 26.6 cm (9 ½ × 10 ½ in.); set of five fabric samples: printed silk, cardboard, 25 × 33 cm (9 ⅞ × 13 in.). Private Collection (126–27)

Design 958. France, 1929. Produced by Metz & Co, 1930. Textile design: gouache, ink, and pencil on paper, 26.9 × 20.9 cm (10 ⅝ × 8 ¼ in.); design card: gouache, ink, and pencil on paper, with silk swatch, 21.4 × 24 cm (8 ½ × 9 ½ in.); fabric sample: printed silk crêpe de chine, 90 × 50 cm (35 ½ × 19 ¾ in.). Private Collection (92–93)

Design 989A. France, 1930. Textile design: gouache, ink, and pencil on paper, 64.7 × 50.2 cm (25 ½ × 19 ¾ in.); design card: gouache, ink and pencil on paper, 21.4 × 24 cm (8 ½ × 9 ½ in.); set of five fabric samples: printed silk, cardboard, 13 × 12 cm (5 ⅛ × 4 ¾ in.). Private Collection (128–29)

Design 965. France, 1930. Produced by Metz & Co. Textile designs: gouache on tracing paper, lined, 32.5 × 49.8 cm (12 ⅞ × 19 ⅝ in.); design card: gouache and pencil on paper, 21.6 × 24.2 cm (8 ½ × 9 ½ in.); 6 fabric samples: printed cotton, 14.5 × 15 cm (5 ¾ × 5 ⅞ in.), 13.5 × 12.5 cm (5 ⅜ × 5 in.), 13 × 12 cm (5 ⅛ × 4 ¾ in.), 11 × 11 cm (4 ⅜ × 4 ⅜ in.), 13.5 × 12 cm (5 ⅜ × 4 ¾ in.), 94 × 89 cm (37 × 35 ⅛ in.). Private Collection (COVER, 132–35)

Design 1044. France, 1930. Produced by Metz & Co, 1931. Textile designs: gouache and pencil on tracing paper, 16.5 × 19.7 cm (6 ½ × 7 ¾ in.), 23.2 × 27.3 cm (9 ⅛ × 10 ¾ in.), 22.2 × 23 cm (8 ¾ × 9 ⅛ in.); 4 fabric samples: printed cotton georgette, 51 × 86 cm (20 ⅛ × 33 ⅞ in.), 15 × 20 cm (5 ⅞ × 7 ⅞ in.), 10 × 15 cm (4 × 5 ⅞ in.), 10 × 15 cm (4 × 5 ⅞ in.). Private Collection (136–37, 198)

Design 1258: six color samples. France, 1933. Gouache and pencil on paper, with fabric swatches, 8.6 × 15.3 cm (3 ⅜ × 6 in.), 6.2 × 17.2 cm (2 ½ × 6 ¾ in.), 6.2 × 15.3 cm (2 ½ × 6 in.), 7.4 × 18.3 cm (3 × 7 ¼ in.), 6.8 × 18.2 cm (2 ¾ × 7 ¼ in.), 7.3 × 16.8 cm (2 ⅞ × 6 ⅝ in.). Private Collection

METZ & AVANT-GARDE DESIGN

Design 4901b. France, 1949. Gouache and pencil on paper, 45 × 73.3 cm (17 ¾ × 28 ⅞ in.). Private Collection (176)

Design 1303. France, 1934. Fabric produced by Metz & Co. Gouache, ink, and pencil on paper, 27 × 20.9 cm (10 ⅝ × 8 ¼ in.). Private Collection (48)

Variation on design 1355. France, 1934. Gouache on paper, 50 × 32.4 cm (19 ¾ × 12 ¾ in.). Private Collection (150)

Design 1176. France, 1933. Produced by Metz & Co, 1934. Gouache on paper, 27.4 × 22.5 cm (10 ⅞ × 8 ⅞ in.). Private Collection (110)

Design 1386. France, 1934. Produced by Metz & Co, 1936. 3 textile designs: gouache, pencil, and ink on paper, 30.3 × 24.7 cm (12 × 9 ¾ in.), 32.6 × 25.2 cm (12 ⅞ × 10 in.), 32.4 × 25.4 cm (12 ¾ × 10 in.); set of four fabric samples: printed silk crêpe de chine, cardboard, 77.5 × 50 cm (30 ½ × 19 ¾ in.). Private Collection (152–53)

Design C53. France, 1924. Gouache and pencil on paper, 36.5 × 28.8 cm (14 ⅜ × 11 ⅜ in.). Private Collection (111)

Design Cbis53. France, 1924. Gouache and pencil on paper, 36.5 × 28.8 cm (14 ⅜ × 11 ⅜ in.). Private Collection

Design A53. France, 1924. Gouache and pencil on paper, 36.5 × 28.8 cm (14 ⅜ × 11 ⅜ in.). Private Collection (112)

Design B53. France, 1924. Gouache and pencil on paper, 36.5 × 28.8 cm (14 ⅜ × 11 ⅜ in.). Private Collection (112)

Design B53 (large version). France, 1924. Gouache on paper, 100 × 75 cm (39 ⅜ × 29 ½ in.). Private Collection (113)

Design B53 (large version 2). France, 1924. Gouache on paper, 100 × 75 cm (39 ⅜ × 29 ½ in.). Private Collection

Design 1389ter. France, 1934. Produced by Metz & Co, 1936. Gouache, pencil, and ink on paper, 30.3 × 24.7 cm (12 × 9 ¾ in.). Private Collection (151)

Design 1177, 10 colorways. France, 1933. Produced by Metz & Co, 1934. Gouache on paper, 22.5 × 20.8 cm (8 ⅞ × 8 ¼ in.), 22.7 × 21 cm (9 × 8 ¼ in.), 22.5 × 20.8 cm (8 ⅞ × 8 ¼ in.), 22.5 × 20.8 cm (8 ⅞ × 8 ¼ in.), 23.6 × 19.5 cm (9 ⅜ × 7 ¾ in.), 22.8 × 21 cm (9 × 8 ¼ in.), 24.8 × 19.4 cm (9 ¾ × 7 ⅝ in.), 23 × 19.5 cm (9 ⅛ × 7 ¾ in.), 48.2 × 19.8 cm (19 × 7 ⅞ in.), 48 × 19.5 cm (18 ⅞ × 7 ¾ in.). Private Collection (122)

Four designs for rugs. Designed by Friedrich Vordemberge-Gildewart (Dutch, born Germany, 1889–1962). The Netherlands, 1939. Gouache on ingrain wallpaper, mounted on cardboard, 33 × 33 cm (13 × 13 in.). Private Collection (109)

Design for a Rug 1. Designed by Georges Vantongerloo (Belgian, 1886–1965). France, 1936. Produced by Metz & Co, 1937. Gouache and ink on cardboard, 15 × 11.1 cm (5 ⅞ × 4 ⅜ in.). Private Collection

Design for a Rug 2. Designed by Georges Vantongerloo (Belgian, 1886–1965). France, 1936. Produced by Metz & Co, 1937. Gouache and ink on cardboard, 15 × 11.1 cm (5 ⅞ × 4 ⅜ in.). Private Collection (108)

Design for a Rug 3. Designed by Georges Vantongerloo (Belgian, 1886–1965). France, 1936. Produced by Metz & Co, 1937. Gouache and ink on cardboard, 15 × 11.1 cm (5 ⅞ × 4 ⅜ in.). Private Collection (108)

Design for a Rug 6. Designed by Georges Vantongerloo (Belgian, 1886–1965). France, 1936. Produced by Metz & Co, 1937. Gouache and ink on cardboard, 14 × 10 cm (5 ½ × 4 in.). Private Collection

Design for a Rug 7. Designed by Georges Vantongerloo (Belgian, 1886–1965). France, 1936. Produced by Metz & Co, 1937. Gouache and ink on cardboard, 14 × 10 cm (5 ½ × 4 in.). Private Collection (108)

Design for a Rug 9. Designed by Georges Vantongerloo (Belgian, 1886–1965). France, 1936. Produced by Metz & Co, 1937. Gouache and ink on cardboard, 14 × 7 cm (5 ½ × 2 ¾ in.). Private Collection

Design for 5 Rugs. Designed by Bart van der Leck. The Netherlands, 1933–34. Pencil and gouache on paper, 55 × 77 cm (21 ⅝ × 30 ⅜ in.). Private Collection

Design for a Rug L2. Designed by Bart van der Leck. The Netherlands, 1918. Produced by Metz & Co, 1929. Gouache and pencil on paper, 37.9 × 28 cm (15 × 11 in.). Private Collection (116)

Design for a Rug L1 Col. B. Designed by Bart van der Leck. The Netherlands, 1918. Produced by Metz & Co, 1929. Gouache and pencil on paper, 32.5 × 25 cm (12 ⅞ × 9 ⅞ in.). Private Collection

Design for a Rug L1. Designed by Bart van der Leck. The Netherlands, 1918. Produced by Metz & Co, 1929. Gouache and pencil on paper, 37.9 × 27 cm (15 × 10 ⅝ in.). Private Collection (116)

Red Blue chair. Designed by Gerrit Rietveld. The Netherlands, ca. 1923. Painted wood, 86.7 × 66 × 83.8 cm (34 ⅛ × 26 × 33 in.); seat h: 33 cm (13 in.). Museum of Modern Art, New York 487.1953, Gift of Philip Johnson (119)

Blocks. France, 1951. Printed linen, 840 × 139 cm (330 ¾ × 54 ¾ in.). Private Collection (202)

Reversible rug. Designed by Bart van der Leck. The Netherlands, 1937, version 1951. 130 × 61 cm (51 ¼ × 24 in.). Private Collection (117)

Color Scheme. Designed by Bart van der Leck. The Netherlands, 1939. Gouache and pencil on paper, 31 × 45 cm (12 ¼ × 17 ¾ in.). Private Collection

Zig-Zag chair. Designed by Gerrit Rietveld. The Netherlands, 1934. Oak, brass fittings, 75 × 36.8 × 44.5 cm (29½ × 14 ½ × 17 ½ in.). Museum of Modern Art, New York 405.1988, Arthur Drexler Fund (118)

Design for a Rug for Metz & Co. Designed by Bart van der Leck. The Netherlands, 1933–39. Gouache and pencil on paper, 19 × 22 cm (7 ½ × 8 ¾ in.). Private Collection

Design for a Rug for Metz & Co. Designed by Bart van der Leck. The Netherlands, 1933–39. Watercolor and pencil on paper, 38.5 × 24.5 cm (15 ¼ × 9 ⅝ in.). Private Collection (116)

Design for a Rug for Metz & Co. Designed by Bart van der Leck. The Netherlands, 1930–39. Watercolor and pencil on paper, 38.5 × 26 cm (15 ¼ × 10¼ in.). Private Collection (116)

Design for a Rug for Metz & Co. Designed by Bart van der Leck. The Netherlands, 1933–39. Gouache and pencil on paper, 17.5 × 8.5 cm (6 ⅞ × 3 ⅜ in.). Private Collection

Red/Blue chair with rounded slats. Gerrit Rietveld. The Netherlands, 1918–23. Aniline graphite pencil on paper, 1:1 scale, 106.7 × 99.5 cm (42 × 39 ¼ in.). Private Collection (119)

Zig-Zag chair (R-18). Gerrit Rietveld. The Netherlands, 1932–34. Pencil and ink on tracing paper, 1:1 scale, 81.1 × 64.2 cm (32 × 25 ¼ in.). Private Collection (118)

Design drawing of Cupboards and Table for Living Room for Metz & Co. Gerrit Rietveld. The Netherlands, 1952. Colored pencil and ink on lined paper, 20.4 × 27.5 cm (8 ⅛ × 10 ⅞ in.). Private Collection (119)

Red/Blue Chair with Rounded Slats. Gerrit Rietveld. The Netherlands, 1918–23. Pencil on tracing paper, 1:10 scale, 22.8 × 29 cm (9 × 11 ½ in.). Private Collection (119)

Zig-Zag Table (R-49) for Metz & Co. Gerrit Rietveld. The Netherlands, 1940. Pencil on tracing paper, 1:10 scale, 27 × 38 cm (10 ⅝ × 15 in.). Private Collection

Zig-Zag armchair (R-46) for Metz & Co. Gerrit Rietveld. The Netherlands, 1940. Pencil and ink on tracing paper, 1:10 scale, 28.5 × 27.6 cm (11 ¼ × 10⅞ in.). Private Collection (118)

Metz & Co design no. M113 set of fabric samples. Designed by Vilmos Huszar (Dutch, born Hungary, 1884–1960). The Netherlands, 1922. Printed silk crêpe de chine, cardboard, 45 × 26.5 cm (17 ¾ × 10 ½ in.). Private Collection

Metz & Co design no. M115 set of fabric samples. Designed by Vilmos Huszar. The Netherlands, 1922. Printed linen, cardboard, 38 × 31 cm (15 × 12 ¼ in.). Private Collection (109)

Metz & Co design no. M116 set of fabric samples. Designed by Vilmos Huszar. Printed by Froment. The Netherlands, 1922. Printed linen, cardboard, 20 × 29.5 cm (7 ⅞ × 11 ⅝ in.). Private Collection

Scarf, Design 593 #3. Produced by Liberty's of London. France, 1969. Printed silk, 85 × 85 cm (33 ½ × 33 ½ in.). Private Collection (182)

Scarf. Produced by Liberty's of London. France, ca. 1967. Printed silk voile, 80 x 80 cm (31 ½ x 31 ½ in.). Private Collection (184)

Scarf. France, date unknown. Printed silk crêpe de chine, 165.1 x 38.1 cm (65 in. x 15 in.). Collection of Andrew Baseman (16)

Design 485. France, 1947. Produced by Metz & Co, 1948. Textile design: gouache and ink on tracing paper, 85 x 85 cm (33 ½ x 33 ½ in.); proof sample: printed wool, 36 x 196 cm (14 ¼ in. x 78 ¼ in.). Private Collection (174)

Design 4903 Rosarium II. France, 1949. Produced by Metz & Co, 1950. Gouache on paper, 54.5 x 42.4 cm (21 ½ x 16 ¾ in.). Private Collection (179)

Design 4902 Rosarium I. France, 1949–50. Studies: gouache and pencil on paper, 58.5 x 39 cm (23 ⅟₁₆ x 15 ⅜ in.); textile design: gouache and pencil on paper, 75 x 52.4 cm (29 ½ x 20 ⅝ in.); fabrics: printed linen, 370 x 130 cm (145 ¾ in. x 51 ¼ in.), 410 x 130 cm (161 ½ in. x 51 ¼ in.). Private Collection (178–81).

Design 1494. France, 1934–36. Gouache on paper, 48 x 31 cm (18 ⅞ x 12 ¼ in.). Private Collection (101)

Design 1493. France, 1934–36. Gouache on paper, 48 x 31 cm (18 ⅞ x 12 ¼ in.). Private Collection (100)

Design 1492, 1492bis. France, 1934–36. Gouache on paper, 48 x 31 cm (18 ⅞ x 12 ¼ in.); 20 x 10 cm (7 ⅞ x 4 in.). Private Collection (99)

Design 1490. France, 1934–36. Gouache and pencil on paper, 48 x 31 cm (18 ⅞ x 12¼ in.). Private Collection (98)

Design 1489. France, 1934–36. Gouache on paper, 30.8 x 23.7 cm (12 ⅛ x 9 ⅜ in.). Private Collection (96)

Design 1488. France, 1934–36. Gouache on paper, 30.8 x 23.8 cm (12 ⅛ x 9 ⅜ in.). Private Collection (96)

Design 1487. France, 1934–36. Gouache on paper, 31 x 23.5 cm (12 ¼ x 9 ¼ in.). Private Collection (97)

Design 1486. France, 1934–36. Gouache on paper, 30.8 x 23.8 cm (12 ⅛ x 9 ⅜ in.). Private Collection (97)

Design 501. France, 1948. Textile design: gouache and pencil on paper, 50 x 60 cm (19 ¾ x 23 ⅝ in.); design card: gouache, ink and pencil on paper, 21.5 x 24.2 cm (8 ½ x 9½in.). Private Collection (175)

Scarf. Produced by Liberty's of London. France, ca. 1967. Printed silk voile, 160 x 43 cm (63 x 17 in.). Private Collection (177)

Scarf. Produced by Liberty's of London. France, ca. 1967. Printed silk voile, 160 x 43 cm (63 x 17 in.). Private Collection (182–83)

Design 1152. France, 1932. Produced by Metz & Co, 1933. Working drawing: gouache and pencil on paper, 49.8 x 32.9 cm (19 ⅝ x 12 ¹⁵⁄₁₆ in.); textile design: gouache and pencil on paper, 23 x 22.5 cm (9 ⅟₁₆ x 8 ⅞ in.); 4 fabric samples: printed silk, 14 x 15.5 cm (5 ½ x 6 ⅛ in.), 12 x 11.5 cm (4 ¾ x 4 ½ in.), 16.5 x 8 cm (6 ½ x 3 ⅛ in.), 15 x 10 cm (5 ⅞ x 4 in.). Private Collection (138–39)

Design 1153. Produced by Metz & Co, 1933. Printed by Petitdidier. France, 1932. Textile design: gouache, ink, and pencil on paper, 14.7 x 20 cm (5 ⅞ x 7 ⅞ in.); master print: colorprint, pencil, and ink on paper, 55.9 x 45 cm (22 x 17 ¾ in.); 6 fabric samples: printed silk, 13 x 14.5 cm (5 ⅛ x 5 ¾ in.), 15 x 18 cm (5 ⅞ x 7 ⅛ in.), 14 x 13.5 cm (5 ½ x 5 ⅜ in.), 15 x 14 cm (5 ⅞ x 5 ½ in.), 12 x 16 cm (4 ¾ x 6 ⅜ in.), 14.5 x 14.5 cm (5 ¾ x 5 ¾ in.). Private Collection (48–49)

Design 1451. France, 1934–36. Gouache on paper, lined, 50 x 33 cm (19 ¾ x 13 in.). Private Collection (110)

Design 1324. France, 1934. Produced by Metz & Co. Printed by Petitdidier. Textile design: gouache and pencil on paper, 32.4 x 32.5 cm (12 ¾ x 12 ¹³⁄₁₆ in.); master print: colorprint, pencil, and ink on paper, 64.4 x 50 cm (25 ⅜ x 19 ¹¹⁄₁₆ in.); design card: gouache, ink, and pencil on paper, 21.4 x 24.2 cm (8 ⁷⁄₁₆ x 9 ½ in.); 8 fabric samples: printed silk, 50 x 90 cm (19 ¾ x 35 ½ in.), 10.5 x 16 cm (4 ⅛ x 6 ⅜ in.), 13 x 9.5 cm (5 ⅛ x 3 ¾ in.), 12 x 17 cm (4 ¾ x 6 ¾ in.), 9 x 11 cm (3 ⅝ x 4 ⅜ in.), 9 x 11 cm (3 5/9 x 4 ⅜ in.), 11 x 11 cm (4 ⅜ x 4 ⅜ in.), 14.5 x 10 cm (5 ¾ x 4 in.). Private Collection (86–87)

Design 1293. France, 1934. Produced by Metz & Co. Sketches: gouache and pencil on paper, 31.5 x 23.5 cm (12 ⅜ x 9 ¼ in.); textile design: gouache, ink, and pencil on paper, lined, 32.5 x 32.2 cm (12 ⅞ x 12 ¾ in.); design card: gouache, ink, and pencil on paper, 21 x 24.2 cm (8 ¼ x 9 ½ in.); 5 fabric samples: printed cotton georgette, 50 x 90 cm (19 ¾ x 35 ½ in.), 13.5 x 15 cm (5 ⅜ x 5 ⅞ in.), 16 x 14 cm (6 ⅜ x 5 ½ in.), 17.5 x 16 cm (6 ⅞ x 6 ⅜ in.), 15 x 18 cm (5 ⅞ x 7 ⅛ in.). Private Collection (148–49)

Design 1146. Produced by Metz & Co, 1933. Printed by Petitdidier. France, 1932. Textile design: gouache, ink, and pencil on paper, 21.1 x 23.8 cm (8 ⅜ x 9 ⅜ in.); master print: colorprint, pencil, and ink on paper, 55.9 x 45 cm (22 x 17 ¾ in.); 5 fabric samples: printed silk, 62 x 85 cm (24 ½ x 33 ½ in.), 11 x 30.5 cm (4 ⅜ x 12 in.), 12.5 x 34 cm (5 x 13 ⅜ in.), 10.5 x 35 cm (4 ⅛ x 13 ¾ in.), 9 x 34 cm (3 ⅝ x 13 ⅜ in.). Private Collection (4-5, 140–41)

Design 1147. France, 1932. Produced by Metz & Co, 1933. Printed by Petitdidier. Sketch: gouache and ink on paper, 26.8 x 20.8 cm (10 ⅝ x 8 ¼ in.); textile design: gouache and pencil on paper, 31.6 x 36 cm (12 ½ x 14 ¼ in.); master print: colorprint, pencil, and ink on paper, 56 x 44.4 cm (22 ⅛ x 17 ½ in.); 4 fabric samples: printed silk, 96 x 49 cm (37 ⅞ x 19 ⅜ in.), 34 x 10 cm (13 ⅜ x 4 in.), 29 x 12.5 cm (11 ½ x 5 in.), 31 x 9 cm (12 ¼ x 3 ⅝ in.). Private Collection (142–43)

Design 253. France, 1928–30. Produced by Metz & Co, 1931. Collage: collage of gouache on tracing paper, lined, 56.2 x 34.2 cm (22 ⅛ x 13 ½ in.); book plate, *Compositions, Couleurs, Idées* (Editions Moreau), colorplate with pencil, 32 x 24.5 cm (12 ⅝ x 9 ⅝ in.); textile design: gouache, ink, and pencil on paper, 44 x 35 cm (17 ⅜ x 13 ¾ in.); design card: gouache, ink, and pencil on paper, 21.6 x 24.1 cm (8 ½ x 9 ½ in.); book plate: colorplate with pencil, 32 x 24.5 cm (12 ⅝ x 9 ⅝ in.); 4 fabric samples: printed cotton mousseline, 13 x 19.4 cm (5 ⅛ x 7 ⅝ in.), 21 x 12 cm (8 ¼ x 4 ¾ in.), 68 x 92 cm (26 ¾ x 36 ¼ in.), 15.5 x 21 cm (6 ⅛ x 8 ¼ in.). Private Collection (94–95)

Design 1317. France, 1934. Textile design: gouache, ink, and pencil on paper, 26.9 x 20.9 cm (10 ⅝ x 8 ¼ in.); 3 working drawings: gouache and ink on tracing paper, 14.7 x 21.2 cm (5 ⅞ x 8 ⅜ in.), 13.6 x 21.3 cm (5 ⅜ x 8 ⅜ in.), 15.5 x 22 cm (6 ⅛ x 8 ¾ in.); design card: gouache, ink, and pencil on paper, 21.4 x 24.2 cm (8 ½ x 9 ½ in.); master print: colorprint, pencil, and ink on paper, 64.4 x 50.3 cm (25 ⅜ x 19 ⅞ in.); fabric sample: printed silk crêpe de chine, 89.5 x 48 cm (35 ¼ x 18 ⅞ in.). Private Collection (163–67)

Design 1464. France, 1934–36. Gouache on paper, 27 x 16 cm (10 ⅝ x 6 ⅜ in.). Private Collection

Design 1189. France, 1929. Produced by Metz & Co, 1933. Printed by Petitdidier. Working drawing: gouache, ink, and pencil on paper, 26.5 x 37.5 cm (10 ½ x 14 ¾ in.); master print: colorprint, pencil, and ink on paper, 55.6 x 44.8 cm (21 ⅞ x 17 ⅝ in.); 6 fabric samples: printed silk, 10 x 35.5 cm (4 x 14 in.), 10 x 27 cm (4 x 10 ⅝ in.), 8.5 x 35 cm (3 ½ x 13 ¾ in.), 11.5 x 30 cm (4 ½ x 11 ⅞ in.), 11.5 x 16.5 cm (4 ½ x 6 ½ in.), 10 x 30 cm (4 x 11 ⅞ in.); tie: printed silk, 143 x 9 cm (56 ⅜ x 3 ⅝ in.). Private Collection (170–73)

Design 1326. France, 1934. Design card: gouache, ink, and pencil on paper, 21.4 x 24.2 cm (8 ½ x 9 ½ in.); 5 fabric samples: printed silk, 90 x 50 cm (35 ½ x 19 ¾ in.), 12.5 x 11 cm (5 x 4 ⅜ in.), 17 x 14.5 cm (6 ¾ x 5 ¾ in.), 11 x 16.5 cm (4 ⅜ x 6 ½ in.), 11.5 x 12.5 cm (4 ½ x 5 in.). Private Collection

Model wearing a Sonia Delaunay swimsuit. France, ca. 1929. Photograph, 23.5 x 17.2 cm (9 ¼ x 6 ¾ in.). Collection of Antoine Blanchette

Design 891 fabric sample. France, 1929. Produced by Metz & Co, 1936. Printed silk crêpe de chine, 49 x 14 cm (19 ⅜ x 5 ½ in.). Private Collection

Design 903 fabric sample. France, 1929. Produced by Metz & Co, 1936. Printed silk crêpe de chine, cardboard, 90.5 x 31.5 cm (35 ⅝ x 12 ⅜ in.). Private Collection (168)

Design 198 fabric samples and bow tie. France, 1927. Produced by Metz & Co, 1936. Printed silk crêpe de chine, 4 fabric samples: 9 x 37 cm (3 ⅝ x 14 ⅝ in.), three at 13.5 x 7.5 cm (5 ⅜ x 3 in.) each; bow tie: 45 x 76 cm (17 ¾ x 30 in.). Private Collection (156–57)

Design 890f fabric samples. France, 1929. Produced by Metz & Co, 1938. Printed silk crêpe de chine on cardboard header, 90 x 33 cm (35 ½ x 13 in.). Private Collection (22–23)

Design 1391. France, 1934. Produced by Metz & Co, 1936. Fabric book: gouache on paper, 45 x 38 cm (17 ¾ x 15 in.); fabric sample: printed silk, 78 x 50 cm (30 ¾ x 19 ¾ in.). Private Collection (154–55)

Design 951bis. France, 1929. Produced by Metz & Co, 1930. Textile design: gouache, ink, and pencil on paper, 21 x 16 cm (8 ¼ x 6 ⅜ in.); fabric samples: printed silk, 31 x 60 cm (12 ¼ x 23 ⅝ in.). Private Collection (130–31)

Design 1219. France, 1933. Produced by Metz & Co. Textile designs: gouache on tracing paper, 20.5 x 22.8 cm (8 ⅛ x 9 in.), 21 x 20.5 cm (8 ¼ x 8 1/8 in.); fabric sample: printed silk mousseline, 45 x 98 cm (17 ¾ x 38 ⅝ in.). Private Collection (146–47)

Design 1257. France, 1933. Produced by Metz & Co. 2 working drawings: gouache, ink, and pencil on paper, 11 x 23.8 cm (4 ⅜ x 9 3/8 in.); 7 x 4 cm (2 ¾ x 1 ⅝ in.); 2 textile designs: gouache on paper, 19.2 x 32.4 cm (7 ⅝ x 12 ¾ in.), 19 x 32.2 cm (7 ½ x 12 ¾ in.); 2 fabric samples: printed silk, 27 x 37 cm (10 ⅝ x 14 ⅝ in.), 37 x 97 cm (14 ⅝ x 38 ¼ in.). Private Collection (144–45)

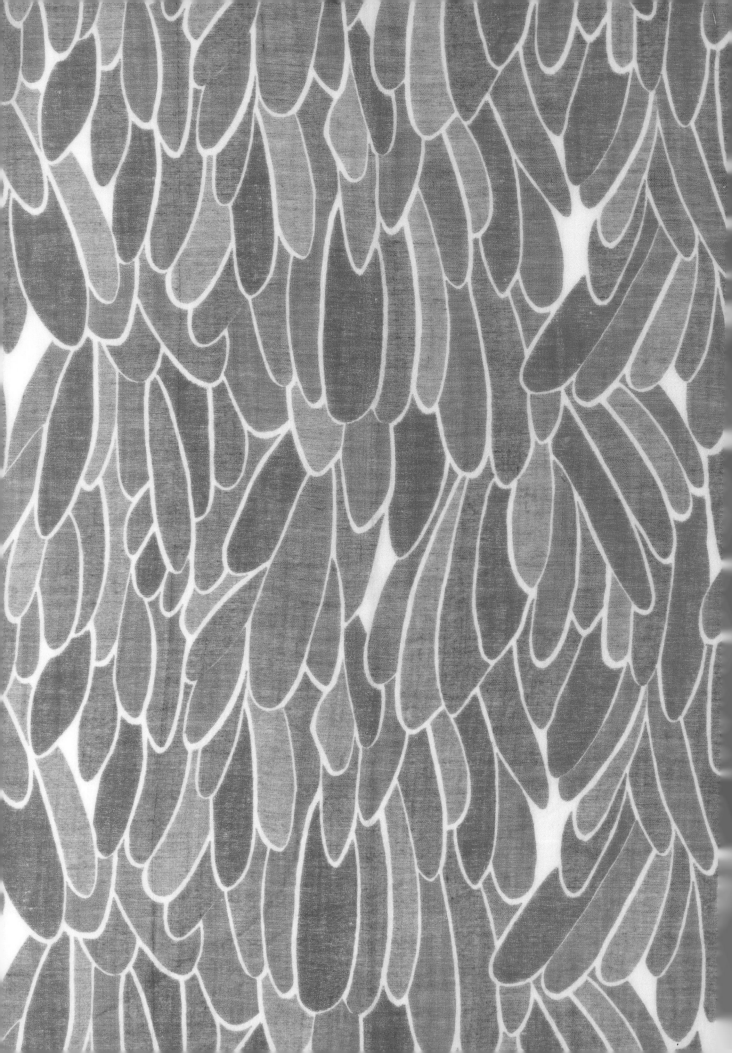

INDEX

ITALICS DENOTE ILLUSTRATIONS

ACKNOWLEDGMENTS

Cooper-Hewitt, National Design Museum is particularly grateful to the following individuals and organizations for their assistance and support during the preparation of the *Color Moves: Art and Fashion by Sonia Delaunay* exhibition and catalogue.

Archives de Paris: Jean-Charles Virmaux, Brigitte Lainé
Art Resource: Jennifer Belt, Kerry Gaertner
Artists Rights Society: Andrea Fisher
Barry Friedman Ltd.: Spencer Tsai
Andrew Baseman
Bibliothèque Nationale de France: Franck Bougamont
Antoine Blanchette
Miriam Gilou Cendrars
Paul André Champagne
Elaine Lustig Cohen
Jean-Louis Delaunay
Folkwang Museum: Ute Eskildsen, Robert Knodt
Kunsthalle Bielefeld: Jutta Hülsewig-Johnen
L & M Services: Anne Quarles
Yoyo Maeght
Metz & Co: Gerard Koolbergen, Jan-Willem Verkruijsen
Musée de l'Impression sur Étoffes: Eric Bellargent,
    Anne-Rose Bringel, Isabelle Dubois-Brinkmann,
    Jacqueline Jacqué, Véronique Lourenço
Musée de la Mode: Sophie Grossiord, Fabienne Falluel
Musée de la Mode Parisienne de Photographie: Sophie Petit
Musée des Arts Décoratifs: Béatrice Salmon,
    Rachel Brishoual, Pamela Golbin, Matthieu Lelièvre,
    Eric Pujalet-Plaa,
Museum of Modern Art: Glenn D. Lowry, Barry Bergdoll,
    Connie Butler, Christophe Cherix, Kathy Curry,
    Paul Galloway, Juliet Kinchin, Jennifer Schauer,
    Gretchen Wagner, Deborah Wye,
Barry Friedman and Patricia Pastor
Richard Riss
Svila Singer
Smithsonian Institution Libraries: Stephen Van Dyk
University of California, Berkeley, Bancroft Library:
    Susan Snyder
    Micah Walter

AT COOPER-HEWITT:

Communications and Marketing: Jennifer Northrop,
    Laurie Olivieri
Conservation: Lucy Commoner, Perry Choe,
    Sarah Scaturro
Curatorial: Cara McCarty, Gregory Herringshaw
Development and External Affairs: Debbie Ahn,
Sophia Amaro, Kate Dobie, Debby Fitzgerald,
    Kelly Gorman, Kelly Mullaney
Education: Caroline Payson, Shamus Adams,
    Kimberly Cisneros, Mei Mah, Marianna Siciliano
Exhibitions: Jocelyn Groom, Matthew O'Connor,
    Mathew Weaver
Finance: Christopher Jeannopoulos
IT: Jimpson Pell, Elvis Reyes
OFEO: Janice Slivko
Publications: Chul R. Kim
Registrar: Steven Langehough, Melanie Fox,
    Wendy Rogers, Bethany Romanowski, Larry Silver
Intern: Jenny Florence

DESIGN TEAM:

Installation design: Toshiko Mori Architect: Toshiko Mori,
    Christy Cheng
Exhibition graphic design: Tsang Seymour Design:
    Catarina Tsang, Patrick Seymour, Elena Penny
Book design: Pure+Applied: Paul Carlos, Kaile Smith
Lighting design: Luce Group: Traci Klainer Polimeni

Tissu simultané no. 205.
France, 1927. Block-printed
on cotton. Musée de l'Impression
sur Étoffes, Mulhouse, 980.563.69

COLOR MOVES:
ART AND FASHION
BY SONIA DELAUNAY

Edited by
Matilda McQuaid
and Susan Brown

with contributions by
Matteo de Leeuw-de Monti
and Petra Timmer

Published by Cooper-Hewitt,
National Design Museum
Smithsonian Institution
2 East 91st Street
New York, NY 10128, USA
WWW.COOPERHEWITT.ORG

Published on the
occasion of the exhibition
Color Moves: Art and
Fashion by Sonia Delaunay
at Cooper-Hewitt,
National Design Museum,
Smithsonian Institution,
March 18–June 5, 2011.

Color Moves: Art and Fashion
by Sonia Delaunay is funded
in part by The Horace W.
Goldsmith Foundation,
The Coby Foundation, Ltd.,
The Anna-Maria and
Stephen Kellen Foundation,
the Ehrenkranz Fund, and
the Esme Usdan Exhibition
Endowment Fund.

**COVER: Design 965
fabric sample.** France,
1930. Produced by
Metz&Co. Printed cotton.
Private collection

**P. 1: Two models
wearing Sonia Delaunay
beachwear, ca. 1927.**
Bibliothèque Nationale de
France, Paris

P.2. Tissu simultané.
France, 1928. Block-
printed silk crêpe de chine.
Musée de l'Impression sur
Étoffes, Mulhouse, 980.585.6

**PP. 4-5. Dessin 1146 fabric
sample.** Produced by Metz
& Co, 1933. Printed by
Petitdidier. France, 1932.
Private collection

**P. 198: Design 1044:
fabric sample.** France,
1930. Produced by Metz
& Co, 1931. Printed cotton
georgette. Private collection

P. 202: Blocks. France, 1951.
Produced by Metz&Co.
Printed linen. Private collection

Additional support is
provided by the Josef and
Anni Albers Foundation,
Lisa S. Roberts, Furthermore:
a program of the J. M. Kaplan
Fund, the Consulate-General
of The Netherlands, and
The Felicia Fund.

This publication is made
possible in part by
The Andrew W. Mellon
Foundation.

Distributed to the trade
in North America by
Distributed Art Publishers
155 Sixth Avenue, 2nd floor
New York, NY 10013, USA
WWW.ARTBOOK.COM

Published outside
North America by
Thames & Hudson Ltd.
WWW.THAMESANDHUDSON.COM

First edition: March 2011

ISBN: 978-0-910503-84-6

Museum Editor: Chul R. Kim,
Director of Publications

Design: Pure+Applied

Printed in the U.S.A.

Library of Congress
Cataloging-in-Publication
Data available from
the publisher.